GOLF JOKES

& EPIC EXCUSES

HILARIOUS REASONS WHY THAT SHOT WASN'T YOUR FAULT

GREENSIDE EDITIONS

TABLE OF CONTENTS

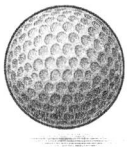

INTRODUCTION

You're standing on the first tee, your buddies watching expectantly, when you proceed to launch your brand-new Pro V1 into what can only be described as a neighboring zip code. As you watch your $5 ball disappear forever into someone's backyard pool, you have two choices:

1. Accept responsibility like a mature adult
2. Blame it on that rogue gust of wind that somehow only affected your ball

If you picked option 2, congratulations—you're already thinking like a true golfer.

Welcome to the wonderful world of golf, a game invented by people who thought hitting a tiny ball into an even tinier hole 400 yards away sounded "relaxing." Somehow, this concept has convinced millions of us that it's a perfectly reasonable way to spend our weekends. And thank goodness for that, because without golf's beautiful chaos, we'd never have developed the fine art of the creative excuse.

THE SCIENCE OF NOT BEING AT FAULT

Here's the thing about golf: it's the only sport where a squirrel can legitimately ruin your entire round, where you can spend more money on gear than some people spend on cars, and where the weather apparently holds personal grudges. In what other activity can you blame your poor performance on everything from the alignment of the golf cart paths to solar flares?

This book isn't about becoming a better golfer—there are plenty of instruction manuals gathering dust on shelves for that noble but futile quest. This is about becoming a *happier* golfer. Because let's face it: you're going to hit bad shots. Your ball is going to find water like it's equipped with sonar. You're going to three-putt from distances that would embarrass a toddler with a plastic club.

But here's the beautiful secret that the golf industry doesn't want you to know: **none of it has to be your fault.**

TRANSFORMING DISASTER INTO COMEDY GOLD

Every golfer has felt that sinking feeling when a perfectly struck shot somehow defies physics, common sense, and basic human decency to end up in the worst possible spot. But what separates the miserable golfers from the memorable ones isn't their handicap—it's their ability to turn catastrophe into comedy.

When you master the art of the golf excuse, something magical happens. That slice into the woods isn't a failure anymore; it's material. That chunked wedge isn't embarrassing; it's entertainment. Suddenly, you're not the guy who can't break 90—you're the guy with the best stories in the clubhouse.

WHY EXCUSES ARE ACTUALLY GENIUS

Before we dive into the good stuff, let's address the elephant in the pro shop: aren't excuses just... well, excuses? Shouldn't we take responsibility for our shots like responsible adults?

To which I say: Have you *met* golf? Golf is a game that will humble a NASA engineer and frustrate a zen master. It's a sport where you can hit the exact same shot twice and get completely different results. If consistency and logic were golf's strong suits, we'd all be scratch players and this book wouldn't exist.

Excuses in golf aren't about avoiding responsibility—they're about maintaining sanity. They're pressure release valves that keep you from throwing your 7-iron into the nearest pond "again". They're social bridges that help you connect with other golfers through shared absurdity. Most importantly, they're reminders that golf is supposed to be *fun*.

YOUR NEW ARSENAL OF AWESOME

In the pages ahead, you'll discover:

- **Classic excuses with modern twists** that will have your playing partners genuinely impressed by your creativity

- **Equipment-based blame strategies** that turn your gear into convenient scapegoats
- **Weather and wildlife explanations** that make Mother Nature your personal nemesis
- **Self-deprecating gems** that somehow make you look better despite admitting you're terrible
- **Quick comebacks** for every disastrous situation the course can throw at you
- **AI vs. Golfer comedy** for the digital age disasters
- **Golf fashion economics** and how to look expensive while playing cheap
- **Interactive excuse challenge** to test how many creative explanations you've already used
- **Real conversation guides** for talking to spouses, bosses, and kids about your golf struggles
- **The deeper philosophy** of why embracing golf's absurdity makes you better at life

A FAIR WARNING

This book comes with one significant side effect: you might actually start enjoying your rounds more. Players have reported increased laughter on the course, improved relationships with playing partners, and a disturbing tendency to look forward to bad shots just to try out new material.

You may also find yourself becoming mysteriously popular in your regular foursome, as people begin requesting to play with "that funny guy who always has the best excuses." Don't say we didn't warn you.

READY TO TEE OFF?

So grab your sense of humor, leave your ego in the parking lot, and prepare to discover why the worst shots often make the best stories. Because in golf, as in life, it's not about what happens to you—it's about how creatively you can blame it on something else.

After all, that shot wasn't your fault.

It never is.

Now let's prove it.

CHAPTER 1:
THE LOST ART OF
THE GOLF EXCUSE

L et me tell you about my friend Dave. Dave takes responsibility for his bad shots.

"Yep, that was all me," he says after chunking a wedge.

The mood dies. The fun evaporates. Dave has turned comedy into group therapy.

Don't be like Dave.

GOLF TRUTH

If you're not blaming squirrels, weather patterns, or cursed clubs—you're doing it wrong.

"Taking responsibility for golf shots is like apologizing to a tornado for standing in its path."

THE ANCIENT ART OF PASSING THE BUCK

Golf excuses are older than your swing coach's advice. Scottish shepherds invented them right after they invented golf.

Old Tom Morris blamed his putting troubles on "wee folk playing tricks."

Bobby Jones threw clubs in creeks, then blamed his caddie's ex-wife for cursing them.

Ben Hogan? "Atmospheric pressure irregularities."

If golf legends can't take blame, why should you?

"Golf excuses: a tradition as old as bad shots."

EXCUSES TOO GOOD NOT TO USE

- "Solar flares affected that trajectory."
- "My ball has abandonment issues with fairways."
- "Clearly a localized magnetic anomaly."
- "That tree definitely moved during my backswing."
- "Atmospheric interference disrupted my swing plane."
- "The earth's rotation threw off my timing."
- "GPS satellites are obviously miscalibrated today."

YOUR BRAIN IS ACTUALLY WIRED FOR THIS

Here's where things get interesting.

Modern psychology tells us that our brains are literally wired to protect our egos through something called "attribution bias." When good things happen, we take credit.

When bad things happen, we blame external factors. This isn't a character flaw—it's a survival mechanism.

In golf terms, this means when you stripe a drive down the middle, your brain happily accepts full credit for your perfect tempo and athletic prowess.

But when that same swing produces a slice that could be tracked by air traffic control, your brain immediately starts scanning for external causes.

"My brain protects my ego better than my short game protects my score."

The wind shifted. The tee was uneven. Someone sneezed in the next county.

"Attribution bias: scientific proof that nothing is ever really your fault."

Fighting this natural tendency is like trying to hold your breath underwater—possible for a while, but ultimately futile and surprisingly exhausting. Smart golfers work *with* their psychology, not against it.

Consider the alternative: accepting blame for every terrible shot means acknowledging that you just spent $60 on green fees to repeatedly demonstrate your incompetence in front of friends. Who needs that kind of honesty? We get enough harsh reality from our credit card statements and bathroom scales.

> *"Golf honesty is overrated—creativity is undervalued."*

 Science supports creative blame-shifting as a legitimate psychological defense mechanism.

THE SOCIAL GLUE OF GOLF EXCUSES

Golf excuses serve another crucial function: they keep the mood light and the friendships intact. When you hit a shot that violates several laws of physics, your playing partners are faced with an awkward social dilemma. Do they commiserate? Offer advice? Pretend they didn't see it?

A well-crafted excuse solves this problem instantly.

> *"That hawk circling overhead created a*
> *downdraft right at impact."*

Instead of tiptoeing around your feelings, your buddies can laugh, share similar stories, and maybe even one-up your creative explanation.

You've transformed an uncomfortable moment into entertainment.

"Wow, Bob, that ball took a hard right like it was avoiding paying taxes!"

"I know, right? I swear that tree jumped out in front of it!"

. . .

And just like that, disaster becomes comedy. The tension breaks, the round continues, and Bob's ego remains intact. Everybody wins.

> *"Good excuses turn golf disasters*
> *into group entertainment."*

Without excuses, golf becomes a series of silent judgments and awkward consolations. With them, it becomes what it was always meant to be: an excuse to spend time with friends while occasionally hitting a ball toward a flag.

 Humor builds stronger friendships than sympathy ever could.

WHAT TO SAY WHEN DISASTER STRIKES

BALL FINDS WATER

- "I'm donating to the aquatic wildlife preservation fund"
- "My ball needed a bath anyway"
- "Testing water temperature for the next group"

· · ·

LOST IN THE TREES

- "My ball needed some shade to think things over"
- "It's exploring the local ecosystem"
- "Tree hugging has gone too far"

· · ·

MASSIVE SLICE

- "I was aiming at the other fairway all along"
- "That's my signature boomerang shot"
- "My ball is socially distancing from the pin"

· · ·

EPIC CHUNK

- "Aerating the fairway for the grounds crew"
- "My divot needed a friend"
- "I'm conducting soil density research"

. . .

COMPLETE WHIFF

- "That was my practice swing, obviously"
- "Just checking the air quality at ball level"
- "My club wanted to experience weightlessness"

WHY "THE WIND DID IT" DOESN'T CUT IT ANYMORE

Here's where most amateur excuse-makers go wrong. They rely on the classics: wind, bad bounces, or "I didn't get all of it." These tired explanations are the golf equivalent of saying "How about them Cowboys?" when conversation lags.

They're safe, predictable, and utterly forgettable.

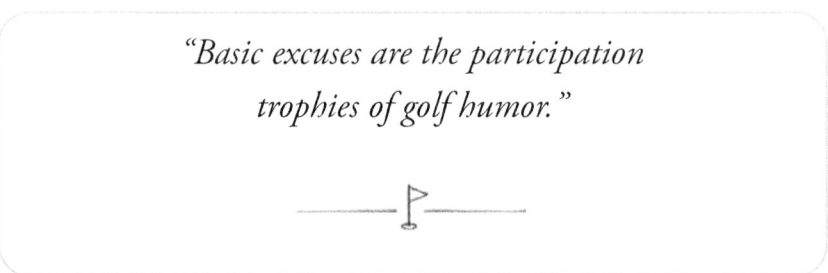

"Basic excuses are the participation trophies of golf humor."

Modern golfers demand better. We live in an age of Netflix specials and viral TikToks. Our entertainment standards have evolved, and so should our excuses.

If you're still blaming routine slices on unpredictable wind patterns, you're basically showing up to a comedy club with knock-knock jokes.

*"Your excuses should be more creative
than your shot selection."*

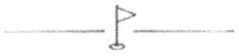

The wind excuse, in particular, has been so overused it's practically meaningless. Unless you're playing in hurricane conditions, claiming wind interference for a shot that traveled 40 yards sideways just makes you look desperate.

OLD AND BUSTED:

- "Bad bounce"
- "Didn't get all of it"
- "The wind caught it"
- "Just a little off"

NEW HOTNESS:

- "A mini-tornado just for my ball."
- "A ninja squad of squirrels sabotaged my shot."
- "A flock of ducks changed my ball's trajectory."
- "The hole shrank just as my ball was about to drop in."

*"Upgrade your excuses like you
upgrade your equipment."*

 *Professional tip: Your excuses should be
10% plausible and 90% entertaining.*

THE EVOLUTION OF EXCUSE EXCELLENCE
THROUGH THE AGES

Golf humor has evolved through distinct eras, each
reflecting the technology and culture of its time. In the
hickory shaft era, golfers blamed bad shots on "inconsistent
wood grain" and "moisture-compromised club integrity."

During the steel shaft revolution, excuses shifted to
"harmonic vibration interference" and "improper weight
distribution."

> *"Every generation of golfers pushes the boundaries of creative blame-shifting."*

1920s: "The wood grain in my mashie is fighting against the natural swing"

1960s: "These steel shafts create resonance patterns that disrupt timing"

1990s: "The graphite composite isn't properly calibrated for my swing speed"

2000s: "GPS interference from cell towers is affecting my club selection"

2020s: "My AI swing coach is experiencing server lag"

2025: "ChatGPT gave me outdated swing advice that's incompatible with my natural motion"

Each generation builds on the work of its predecessors, creating increasingly sophisticated explanations for the same basic problem: hitting a small ball with a stick is really, really hard.

"Excuse innovation never stops—unlike my putting improvement."

 The sophistication of golf excuses has increased exponentially with technology.

SITUATION-SPECIFIC SOLUTIONS
FOR MODERN LIFE

Playing with your boss:

- "Market volatility is affecting my concentration"

- "The quarterly projections threw off my swing tempo"

- "I'm still processing those budget numbers from yesterday's   meeting"

· · ·

Playing with your spouse:

- "The mortgage refinancing stress is getting to me"

- "I was thinking about your honey-do list during my backswing"

- "That conversation about vacation planning disrupted my pre-shot routine"

· · ·

Playing with strangers:

- "I'm still adjusting to the local gravitational field variations"
- "Different time zone is messing with my circadian rhythm timing"
- "The altitude change from my home course is affecting club selection"

· · ·

Playing with teenagers:

- "Your TikTok generation energy is throwing off my millennial swing mechanics"
- "I'm not used to this level of social media pressure during golf"

BUILDING YOUR PERSONAL EXCUSE STYLE

Every golfer needs to develop their own excuse personality. Are you the analytical type who blames shots on complex meteorological phenomena? The storyteller who creates elaborate narratives about vengeful golf balls? The conspiracy theorist who suspects the course maintenance crew has it out for you?

Your excuse style should reflect your actual personality while amplifying it for comedic effect.

"Your excuse persona should be like your golf swing—uniquely yours and slightly exaggerated."

If you're naturally reserved, becoming the golfer with increasingly paranoid theories about equipment sabotage can be hilariously unexpected. If you're already dramatic, leaning into elaborate stories about cosmic interference can be perfectly on-brand.

The worst thing you can do is try to copy someone else's excuse style. A naturally serious person attempting to channel Robin Williams rarely works. Better to find your own voice and develop it over time.

"Authenticity in excuse-making beats imitation every time."

The best excuse-makers are method actors who believe their own explanations.

REAL-LIFE APPLICATIONS BEYOND GOLF

AT THE GROCERY STORE: "I practice putting in the cereal aisle—Cheerios on one side, milk on the other. It's working about as well as you'd expect."

. . .

EXPLAINING YOUR SCORE TO YOUR WIFE: "Honey, I took more steps than swings. That should count as cardio, not as a loss!"

. . .

AT WORK AFTER A BAD ROUND: "Golf taught me valuable lessons about accepting variables beyond my control—like quarterly projections and this morning's coffee quality."

. . .

ORDERING DRINKS AT THE 19TH HOLE: "I need something stronger than my excuses and smoother than my swing. Make it a double."

. . .

TALKING TO YOUR GOLF INSTRUCTOR: "I've been implementing your advice, but I think my clubs are experiencing compatibility issues with the new techniques."

. . .

"Golf excuses work everywhere—the course just provides the training ground."

 Master golf excuses and you've mastered life excuses.

TOMORROW'S EXCUSES TODAY

TECHNOLOGY-FORWARD EXPLANATIONS:

- "SpaceX launch disrupted local gravitational field consistency"

- "My smart ball is having connectivity issues with the course Wi-Fi"

- "ChatGPT's latest update gave me swing advice that's incompatible with reality"

- "The metaverse is glitching and affecting my real-world physics"

- "My carbon footprint offset calculations threw off my balance at address"

• • •

SOCIAL MEDIA AGE EXCUSES:

- "YouTube's algorithm recommended tutorials… for mini-golf!"

- "My swing went viral for all the wrong reasons and now it's self-conscious"

- "LinkedIn notifications during my backswing disrupted my professional composure"

. . .

EMERGENCY EXCUSE KIT

Keep These Ready

For any golf disaster, you need backup explanations:

EQUIPMENT MALFUNCTION:

"My clubs are experiencing technical difficulties"

. . .

WILDLIFE INTERFERENCE:

"That squirrel coordinated a perfectly timed distraction"

. . .

MAGNETIC FIELD DISRUPTION:

"Underground utility cables are affecting iron performance"

. . .

QUANTUM PHYSICS VIOLATION:

"The laws of physics don't apply consistently on this hole"

"A golfer without backup excuses is like a carpenter without extra nails."

THE EXCUSE THAT KEEPS ON GIVING

The beauty of a well-crafted golf excuse is its shelf life. A good excuse doesn't just explain one bad shot—it becomes part of your golfing mythology. Years later, your buddies will still be referencing "that time you blamed your slice on the International Space Station passing overhead."

These become the stories that define your golf persona and keep you invited back to regular games. Nobody remembers your actual scores, but everyone remembers your creative explanations for why those scores weren't your fault.

"Your golf legacy isn't built on scores—it's built on stories."

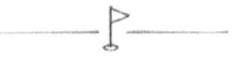

And here's the real secret: the more elaborate and entertaining your excuses become, the less anyone cares about your actual golf performance.

You transition from being "Steve, who shoots 95" to "Steve, who has the funniest explanations for why he shoots 95."

That's a much better reputation to have.

"Entertainment value trumps scoring ability every single time."

The future of golf excuses is bright. As technology advances, so do our opportunities for creative blame-shifting.

Smartwatches can now blame bad shots on elevated heart rates. GPS devices provide exact wind speeds for meteorological   excuses.

Launch monitors give us spin rates and ball speed data to explain why shots didn't perform as expected.

The modern golfer has more excuse-making tools at their disposal than ever before. The only question is: are you creative enough to use them?

> *In the end, it's not about what happens to you—it's about how creatively you can explain why it wasn't your fault.*

CHAPTER 1 TRUTH BOMB

Golf without excuses is just public humiliation with scorecards. Master the art of creative blame-shifting, and you'll never have a bad round again—just rounds with interesting explanations.

Your equipment will betray you.

Weather will conspire against you. Physics will abandon you. Your playing partners will witness disasters that defy rational explanation.

But your excuses? They'll never let you down.

Remember: in golf, as in life, it's not about what happens to you—it's about how creatively you can explain why it wasn't your fault. And trust me, with the right approach, it never has to be your fault again.

> *"Your reputation isn't built on your handicap—*
> *it's built*
> *on your comebacks."*

Ready to test your excuse arsenal? Before we dive into Mother Nature's conspiracy against golfers, flip ahead to the **Golf Excuse Challenge** and see how many creative explanations you've already mastered. Don't worry—if you score low, the next chapters will have you covered with enough blame-shifting ammunition to handle any golf disaster the universe throws at you.

GOLF EXCUSE CHALLENGE

How Many of These Have You Used?

THE ULTIMATE GOLF EXCUSE ACCOUNTABILITY TEST

Instructions: *Check off every excuse you've actually used on the golf course—be honest!*

Weather & Atmospheric Excuses

☐ The wind changed at the last second

☐ The sun was in my eyes

☐ Bad lie in the rough

☐ The course was too wet/too dry

☐ My swing doesn't work in this heat/cold

Wildlife & Surroundings Excuses

☐ Somebody coughed or made noise in my backswing

☐ A bird flew over and distracted me

☐ A bug got in my face right before I swung

☐ Too much movement around me

☐ Course workers or a cart distracted me

Equipment Betrayal Excuses

☐ I used the wrong club

☐ This ball is too old—no life left in it

☐ This new ball doesn't feel right yet

☐ My driver just isn't working today

☐ My glove slipped and ruined my grip

Course Design Sabotage Excuses

☐ The pin placement is unfair

☐ Those trees shouldn't even be there

☐ That was an unlucky bounce "sprinkler head, cart path, etc."

☐ The greens are way too fast/too slow

☐ That bunker sand was impossible—too soft or too hard

Classic Catch-All Excuses

☐ My swing tempo was off

☐ I didn't warm up properly

☐ I lined up wrong without noticing

☐ Total mental lapse

☐ Just bad luck—that's golf

Advanced Psychological Excuses

☐ I was overconfident after that last good shot

☐ The pressure of witnesses affected my performance

☐ I psyched myself out overthinking the shot

☐ My muscle memory is fighting my swing thoughts

☐ I'm having an identity crisis with my swing plane

Technology Malfunction Excuses

☐ My GPS watch malfunctioned mid-swing

☐ The range finder gave me the wrong yardage

☐ My phone buzzed during my backswing

☐ The golf app crashed and confused my club selection

☐ Bluetooth interference from the cart's sound system

YOUR EXCUSE MASTERY SCORECARD

Count up your checks and discover your excuse expertise   level:

0-5 Excuses Used

"THE GOLF SAINT"

Impressive restraint! You either have supernatural self-control or you've successfully blocked out traumatic golf memories. Consider seeing a therapist—either for your abnormal honesty or your repressed golf trauma.

6-10 Excuses Used

"FLUENT IN GOLFERESE"

Respectable excuse vocabulary! You understand that golf requires creative explanations for inexplicable results. You're officially bilingual: English and Golf Excuse.

11-20 Excuses Used

"EXCUSE LEGEND"

Outstanding creativity! You've achieved legendary status in the ancient art of golf blame-shifting. You've used more excuses than most people have golf balls, and that's genuinely impressive.

21-30 Excuses Used

"PROFESSIONAL EXCUSE ARTIST"

You're basically a golf excuse sommelier—sophisticated, experienced, and capable of matching the perfect excuse to any disaster. Your creativity rivals your inability to hit fairways.

30+ Excuses Used

"EXCUSE HALL OF FAMER"

Congratulations! You've transcended normal excuse-making and entered the realm of excuse artistry. You should offer masterclasses in creative golf blame-shifting. Your excuse game is stronger than your actual game, and that's exactly how it should be.

REMEMBER:

The goal isn't to convince anyone your excuses are true—it's to entertain everyone while preserving your dignity. Mission accomplished if people are laughing WITH you, not AT you.

CHAPTER 2:
MOTHER NATURE'S PERSONAL VENDETTA

WHEN THE UNIVERSE CONSPIRES
AGAINST YOUR GOLF GAME

I f you've ever felt like the entire natural world has formed a conspiracy against your golf game, congratulations—you're paying attention. Golf is the only sport where squirrels qualify as legitimate tactical threats and trees seem to have personal vendettas against your scorecard.

Mother Nature doesn't just create obstacles for golfers—she actively auditions them. Trees volunteer for ball-catching duty with suspicious enthusiasm. Water hazards relocate themselves overnight to more strategic positions. Even the grass develops mood disorders.

"Golf: where nature gets revenge for all those perfectly manicured lawns."

"I don't have bad luck—I have a meteorology problem."

The evidence is overwhelming once you start paying attention. That puddle on an otherwise bone-dry fairway? Strategic placement. The sudden wind gust during your backswing? Targeted harassment. That bee that decides to buzz around your head right when you're lining up your shot? It's definitely working with the course management.

> ### GOLF TRUTH
>
> *Weather becomes personal the*
> *moment you tee up.*

SEASONAL WEATHER COMEDY

SPRING:

"Pollen season turns my golf ball into a fuzzy yellow tennis ball mid-flight."

SUMMER:

"It's so hot, my ball is sweating before I even hit it."

FALL:

"The leaves aren't falling—they're jumping out to block my shots."

WINTER:

"My ball is wearing thermals and still complaining about the cold."

WILDLIFE INTELLIGENCE NETWORK

Squirrels: Nature's Tiny Terrorists

Squirrels aren't cute woodland creatures—they're furry operatives running sophisticated psychological warfare campaigns. These bushy-tailed saboteurs have turned golf course harassment into an art form.

> *"Squirrels: the only animals that critique your swing form."*
>
>

Watch one during your pre-shot routine. Perfect timing. Strategic positioning. Military-grade distraction techniques. They're basically conducting a master class in "How to Destroy a Golfer's Concentration 101."

> *"That squirrel just took notes on my backswing and texted them to his supervisor."*
>
>

The worst part? They're judgment-proof. Try explaining to your foursome that a 2-ounce rodent is responsible for your triple bogey. Go ahead. We'll wait.

"I'm being outplayed by something that stores nuts for a living."

SQUIRREL BEHAVIOR ANALYSIS:

- Appears during important shots only
- Vanishes during practice swings
- Makes eye contact during your backswing
- Clearly understands golf scoring better than you do

"Squirrels have never three-putted in their entire existence."

SQUIRREL FACT: *They've mastered golf psychology without ever holding a club.*

Birds: The Aerial Comedy Division

Birds represent nature's air force, but they're also golf's inadvertent comedy writers. They time their appearances with the precision of professional entertainers and the subtlety of a marching band.

"Birds have better course management than most golfers."

Ever notice how they always appear during your most crucial shots? It's like they have season tickets to your personal golf disaster show.

"That hawk has been following our group for three holes—I think we're his entertainment."

Bird Behavioral Patterns:

- Hawks circle overhead during approach shots "intimidation tactics"

- Geese honk disapprovingly at poor putting

- Robins chirp sarcastic commentary after bad drives

- Crows actually laugh at your swing

> *"My golf game is so bad, even the birds are giving me unsolicited advice."*

The timing is always suspicious. Dead silence during practice swings, then a full avian symphony right as you start your downswing.

> *"I need to hire a bird whisperer to negotiate a ceasefire."*

 BIRD FACT: *They've never needed a mulligan.*

Quick Nature Joke Collection

- "Trees: the only audience that never applauds your good shots"
- "Water hazards: where golf balls go to die and golfers go to cry"
- "Sand traps: beaches without the relaxation"
- "Rough: where golf balls go to hide from their shame"
- "Fairways: mythical strips of grass that exist mostly in theory"

UNDERGROUND RESISTANCE MOVEMENT

Moles, gophers, and other subterranean insurgents operate the most sophisticated tunnel network since the Underground Railroad.

These invisible enemies specialize in making perfectly good lies suddenly unstable.

> *"I'm not playing golf—I'm conducting archaeological excavations one divot at a time."*

They work the night shift, creating air pockets and loose soil precisely where you'll take your morning stance. It's like they have access to your tee time reservations.

"The mole union has clearly studied my playing patterns."

UNDERGROUND OPERATIONS INCLUDE:

- Strategic tunnel placement beneath tee boxes
- Precision soil loosening in fairway landing areas
- Advanced divot preparation services
- Coordinated stance destabilization projects

"I need ground-penetrating radar more than I need swing lessons."

The worst part? You can't see them, can't catch them, and can't prove they exist. It's the perfect crime against golf.

"Somewhere underground, there's a mole
keeping statistics on my mishits."

UNDERGROUND FACT:

Moles have better course knowledge
than most caddies.

BOTANICAL WARFARE DIVISION

Trees: Nature's Defensive Line

Trees on golf courses aren't passive obstacles—they're active participants in your scoring struggles. Some have clearly developed magnetic personalities that attract golf balls with supernatural efficiency.

"That oak tree hasn't missed a ball all
season—it should be on tour."

Watch your ball's flight path toward a tree. Physics says it should go straight. Golf reality says the tree will somehow extend its gravitational field and pull your shot directly into its trunk.

"Trees: the only athletes with a 100% interception rate."

TREE DEFENSIVE STRATEGIES:

- Magnetic bark technology for ball attraction
- Strategic branch positioning for maximum ball deflection
- Root system expansion to destabilize nearby lies
- Seasonal leaf deployment for visual obstruction

"I've never seen a tree miss a golf ball—they have better hands than most wide receivers."

The truly advanced trees have learned to coordinate their attacks. One tree deflects your shot toward another, creating pinball-like ricochets that defy multiple laws of physics simultaneously.

> *"It's like playing golf in a pinball machine designed by vindictive landscapers."*

 TREE FACT: *They've never been penalized for interference.*

Grass: The Mood Ring of Golf

Golf course grass has more personality disorders than a reality TV show cast. One minute, it's supporting your ball like a loyal friend; the next, it's creating bounces that belong in a carnival funhouse.

> *"This grass clearly woke up on the wrong side of the sprinkler system."*

GRASS MOOD INDICATORS:

- **Happy grass:** Provides perfect lies and predictable bounces

- **Angry grass:** Creates sideways hops and inexplicable roll patterns

- **Depressed grass:** Swallows balls in lies that look perfect from above

- **Manic grass:** Launches balls in random directions with excessive enthusiasm

"I need a grass whisperer more than a swing coach."

The most frustrating grass is the passive-aggressive variety. It looks perfect, feels perfect, then produces a ball reaction that violates everything you know about physics and geometry.

"This turf has trust issues with golf balls."

 GRASS FACT: *It has better mood swings than most golfers.*

COURSE MAINTENANCE CONSPIRACY: THE GROUNDS CREW PLOT

Golf course maintenance crews wake up each morning asking themselves one question: "How can we make today more difficult for golfers?" These turf terrorists disguise their sabotage as "course improvement."

> *"The grounds crew is clearly working for the other team."*

MAINTENANCE TIMING CONSPIRACY:

- Aerate greens right before your round
- Water fairways during your backswing
- Mow rough while you're trying to concentrate
- Fill divots with concrete instead of sand

> *"Course maintenance timing is suspiciously coordinated with my tee times."*

The grounds crew has perfected the art of making course conditions change between your practice swing and actual shot. The grass you practiced on mysteriously becomes different grass when it matters.

"They replaced my perfect lie with a different lie while I was selecting my club."

The Sprinkler Head Alliance

Sprinkler heads are strategically placed by maintenance crews to create the maximum number of unlucky bounces. These metal disc deflectors have a magnetic attraction to well-struck golf balls.

"Sprinkler heads have better defensive statistics than most NFL linebackers."

SPRINKLER HEAD CONSPIRACY EVIDENCE:

- Perfect shots that hit sprinklers and carom into hazards
- Balls that find every sprinkler head on the course

- Sprinkler heads that seem to move between rounds
- Underground irrigation designed for maximum ball interference

> *The sprinkler system doubles as a ball-deflection network."*

Grounds Crew Sabotage Tactics

"The mowers leave tire tracks exactly where my ball wants to roll"

• • •

"They move the tee markers overnight to mess with my alignment"

• • •

"The grounds crew has a betting pool on how many balls I'll lose"

• • •

"Course maintenance is really course sabotage disguised as improvement"

• • •

"They cut the rough shorter everywhere except where my ball lands"

WATER HAZARD PSYCHOLOGY

Lakes, Ponds, and Streams: Golf Ball Graveyards

Water hazards possess gravitational forces that exceed their actual size by approximately 3,000%. A tiny creek somehow attracts golf balls from distances that would make NASA jealous.

> *"Water hazards: where physics goes to die and golf balls go to disappear."*

WATER HAZARD PSYCHOLOGICAL PROFILES:

- **Ponds:** Passive-aggressive collectors with deceptively calm surfaces

- **Streams:** Active hunters that chase balls across fairways

- **Lakes:** Professional archives maintaining permanent golf ball collections

- **Fountains:** Show-offs that add insult to injury with decorative splashing

"I've donated so many balls to water hazards,
I should get a tax deduction."

The most diabolical water hazards are the ones that look innocent. A tiny stream that seems easily clearable suddenly develops the gravitational pull of a black hole when your ball approaches.

"That creek is only six inches deep, but it
swallows golf balls like a hungry hippo."

Water hazards also have perfect timing. They remain invisible during practice swings, then materialize precisely where your ball decides to land.

"Water hazards are basically Bermuda
Triangles for golf equipment."

WATER FACT: *They have better collection rates than the IRS.*

Quick Water Hazard Jokes

"I'm single-handedly keeping the golf ball manufacturing industry profitable"

• • •

"My balls have found more water than a professional well-digger"

• • •

"That pond has more of my equipment than my golf bag"

• • •

"I'm creating an underwater golf museum one shot at a time"

• • •

GOLF COURSE MAINTENANCE

The Conspiracy

Pin Placements: Strategic Torture

Golf course maintenance crews wake up each morning asking themselves: "Where can we put today's pins to maximize human suffering?" These placement specialists have turned flag positioning into psychological warfare.

> *"Pin placement committees clearly*
> *moonlight as professional torturers."*

DAILY PIN PLACEMENT STRATEGIES:

- Behind bunkers "maximum approach shot difficulty"
- On slopes "gravity-defying putt requirements"
- In corners "geometric impossibility challenges"
- Near water "psychological intimidation tactics"

> *"Today's pins are located in alternate dimensions*
> *where normal physics don't apply."*

The most sadistic pins are placed exactly where they look reasonable from the tee but reveal their true evil nature only after you've committed to your approach shot.

> *"That pin placement violates the Geneva Convention guidelines for fair play."*

PRO SHOP CONVERSATION:

"Where's today's pin on 12?" "About three inches left of impossible and two feet short of ridiculous."

PIN PLACEMENT FACT: *They're positioned by people who've clearly given up on human happiness.*

GRAVITY MALFUNCTIONS:

When Physics Goes Rogue

Golf balls operate under different gravitational rules than every other object on the planet.

Regular physics suggests that what goes up must come down in predictable patterns.

Golf physics suggests that what goes up will find the most inconvenient place to come down.

> *"My ball discovered a wormhole between the tee and the fairway."*

GRAVITY ANOMALY INDICATORS:

- Balls that curve mid-air without wind assistance
- Perfect shots that suddenly drop straight down
- Shots that gain altitude after hitting the ground
- Balls that seem to hover over water hazards before diving in

*"Apparently gravity works differently when
golf balls are involved."*

The most frustrating gravity malfunctions are the ones that affect only your ball while leaving your playing partners' shots subject to normal physics.

*"Everyone else's ball obeys Newton's laws. Mine
operates under Murphy's laws."*

COMMON GRAVITY EXCUSES:

- "Localized gravitational field disturbance"
- "That shot encountered a density pocket"
- "The earth's rotation affected my ball trajectory"
- "Solar gravity interfered with the shot"

*"I need NASA to study the physics
around my golf ball."*

Physics Malfunction Menu

"My ball violated three laws of physics on that shot"

. . .

"Gravity apparently has a personal vendetta against my scorecard"

. . .

"The laws of physics don't apply consistently to my golf game"

. . .

"I'm experiencing gravitational discrimination"

. . .

"My ball thinks it's on Jupiter where everything falls faster"

. . .

CHAPTER 2 TRUTH BOMB

Mother Nature has been running a 150-year psychological experiment on golfers, and the results are conclusive: environmental factors will always find new ways to interfere with your golf shots.

She has unlimited resources, home field advantage, and millions of years of experience in making life difficult for humans wielding expensive sticks.

But here's the beautiful truth: recognizing this environmental conspiracy isn't paranoia—it's tactical awareness.

Once you understand that weather, wildlife, and landscaping are actively working against your golf success, you can stop taking it personally and start appreciating the comedy.

The weather will always surprise you at the worst possible moment. Squirrels will continue their surveillance operations. Trees will maintain their perfect interception record. Water hazards will keep expanding their golf ball collections.

And you know what? That's exactly what makes golf the most entertainingly frustrating sport ever invented.

"Nature started this war, but we have the last laugh through superior storytelling abilities."

Next up: When your own equipment joins the enemy coalition...

AI'S GUIDE TO GOLF IMPOSSIBILITY

ARTIFICIAL INTELLIGENCE FINALLY MEETS
ARTIFICIAL CONFIDENCE

AI CADDIE SIMULATOR

Golfer: "Which club should I use on this hole?"
ChatGPT: "An umbrella… your swing always brings a storm."

Golfer: "How do I read this green?"
ChatGPT: "With augmented reality glasses… or a lot of faith."

Golfer: "Should I risk it with the driver?"
ChatGPT: "Sure, that way you'll have a reason to buy the next one."

Golfer: "What's my best strategy here?"
ChatGPT: "Aim for the water. That way, if you miss, at least you hit your target."

Golfer: "Any tips for concentration?"
ChatGPT: "Turn off your phone… and also your current swing."

AI GOLF PREDICTIONS

Golfer: "Will I improve this year?"

ChatGPT: "Yes, in your ability to come up with excuses."

Golfer: "How far will my drive go?"

ChatGPT: "Far enough to lose it, but not far enough to brag about it."

Golfer: "What score will I shoot today?"

ChatGPT: "A world record... for most balls lost."

Golfer: "Will I make a birdie on this hole?"

ChatGPT: "Yes, but only at mini-golf."

Golfer: "Will I finally break 90 this season?"

ChatGPT: "Absolutely... if you only count the holes where you didn't lose a ball."

CHAPTER 3:
THE GOLF SHOPPING
ADDICTION

G olf is the only sport where you can spend more money on gear than some people spend on cars, and still play worse than when you started. It's a beautiful, expensive trap: every bad shot convinces you that better equipment is the answer.

The golf industry has perfected the art of selling hope in titanium packages.

"A new driver will fix my slice... this time."

"These irons are designed for players like me...
players who blame their clubs."

Welcome to the endless cycle of golf spending, where logic goes to die and credit cards go to cry.

GOLF TRUTH:
The worse you play, the more expensive
your gear becomes.

Equipment Shopping Logic

- "This club is on sale... I'm actually saving money"
- "I need backup clubs in case my regular ones stop working"
- "If the pros use it, it must be the difference maker"
- "My swing will improve once I have the right equipment"
- "These clubs are an investment in my future golf success"

GOLF FASHION

LOOKING EXPENSIVE WHILE PLAYING CHEAP

The Polo Shirt Economy

Golf is the only sport where you can miss a one-foot putt while dressed like you're on a fashion runway. Your outfit costs more than most people's entire weekend entertainment budget.

*"You know you're a golfer when your polo shirt
costs more than your family dinner."*

GOLF FASHION ECONOMICS:

- Polo shirts: $80-150 "to look professional while playing   amateur"

- Golf pants: $120-200 "so your disasters look stylish"

- Golf shoes: $200-400 "for walking in expensive shame"

- Total fashion investment: More than your car payment

*"Golf clothing promises to improve your swing... the
only thing it improves is your credit card bill."*

The cruel irony is that looking like a professional golfer doesn't make you play like one. But at least your three-putts will be well-dressed.

*"If elegance counted toward handicap,
I'd already be scratch."*

Golf fashion operates on the theory that if you look expensive enough, people won't notice how badly you're playing. Unfortunately, scorecards don't have style points.

> *"In golf, the more ridiculous your pants, the better your excuse for playing badly."*

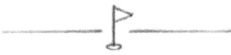

FASHION TRUTH:
Looking like a pro and playing like a pro require completely different budgets.

The Accessories Arms Race

Golf accessories are where fashion meets desperation. Every golfer needs the complete ensemble to look the part, even if they can't play the part.

ESSENTIAL ACCESSORIES BUDGET:

- Golf hat/visor: $30-60 "sun protection for outdoor embarrassment"
- Golf glove: $15-25 per glove "grip enhancement for grip failures"
- Golf towel: $20-40 "to wipe away tears and ball marks"
- Divot tool: $15-30 "for the rare occasions you actually hit the ground after the ball"

> *"My golf accessories cost more than my first apartment's monthly rent."*

The accessories promise performance enhancement but deliver only the appearance of knowing what you're doing.

> *"I have every golf accessory except the one that matters: actual skill."*

Golf Fashion Reality Check

I dress like I can break 80... I play like I can barely break 100"

"My outfit suggests country club membership; my swing suggests miniature golf experience"

"I look professional from the tee box, amateur from the scorecard"

"Golf fashion: where $500 outfits meet $5 golf abilities"

"My wardrobe has more style than my short game has substance"

HOW TO SPOT A BAD GOLFER

THE EQUIPMENT EDITION

The Over-Equipped Underperformer

Bad golfers can be identified by the inverse relationship between equipment quality and actual performance. The more expensive the gear, the more creative the excuses need to be.

> *"The one who says, 'I played great... the ball just didn't cooperate.'"*

CLASSIC BAD GOLFER INDICATORS:

- Wears new gloves, new shoes, new cap... and still loses every ball

- Spends more time preparing for the shot than actually missing it

- Perfect practice swings; the real swing is a natural disaster

- Talks endlessly about equipment specs until it's time to perform

"Perfect practice swings followed by swing disasters—the classic bad golfer signature move."

The bad golfer believes that the right equipment will unlock their hidden potential. The hidden potential remains very well hidden.

"Starts every story with, 'I used to play well...' and you already know the ending involves expensive solutions."

The Equipment Excuse Master

Bad golfers develop sophisticated explanations for why expensive gear isn't producing expensive results.

"These clubs are still learning my swing style."

"This ball doesn't match my club specifications."

"My equipment is too advanced for this course's conditions."

The equipment excuse master can turn any gear malfunction into a reason why poor performance isn't their fault.

"My clubs are optimized for different atmospheric conditions than what we're experiencing today."

 **BAD GOLFER IDENTIFICATION:** *The more they blame equipment, the more equipment they own.*

Bad Golfer Equipment Behaviors

"Adjusts club settings between every shot but never adjusts expectations"

"Carries more clubs than a pro shop but uses them like a beginner"

"Reads equipment reviews like they're studying for finals"

"Has strong opinions about gear performance despite consistent poor results"

"Believes the next purchase will be the game-changer"

THE EQUIPMENT SPENDING SPIRAL

The New Driver Delusion

Every golfer believes their next driver purchase will be the one that finally fixes their slice. This belief persists despite overwhelming evidence to the contrary.

"A new driver: $500. The same old slice: free."

DRIVER PURCHASE CYCLE:

- Month 1: Research the "perfect" driver

- Month 2: Purchase with high expectations
- Month 3: Initial optimism meets reality
- Month 4: Blame the shaft, grip, or loft settings
- Month 5: Start researching the next "perfect" driver

*"I've bought more drivers than a taxi company
and still can't find the fairway."*

The driver delusion is powered by golf marketing that promises distance, accuracy, and forgiveness. What it delivers is mostly buyer's remorse.

*"My driver collection is worth more than my
car, and my car actually goes where I point it."*

The Putter Paranoia

Putting problems lead to putter purchases with religious frequency. Every missed putt must be the putter's fault, not the golfer's read, speed, or stroke.

"Changing your putter every season: expensive.
Still missing from three feet: priceless."

Putter Purchase Patterns:

- Blade putters for "feel" "that you can't feel"

- Mallet putters for "forgiveness" "that doesn't forgive"

- Insert putters for "roll" "that still rolls past the hole"

- Expensive putters for "confidence" "that disappears with the first miss"

"I have more putters than a miniature golf course
and less accuracy than a blindfolded child."

The putter paranoia assumes that the right flat stick will solve putting problems that are fundamentally about reading greens and controlling distance.

"My putter budget exceeds most people's entire
golf equipment investment."

> ### SPENDING TRUTH:
> *The more putters you own, the more putting problems you acknowledge.*

Equipment Budget Reality

"Golf is the only sport where you think new clubs are cheaper than lessons... until you buy the clubs"

"My bag has more irons than a hardware store and performs about the same"

"I've spent so much on equipment that playing badly on purpose would at least be cheaper"

"The rule of modern golf: equipment quality is inversely proportional to golf ability"

"I could have bought a small car for what I've spent on drivers alone"

WHEN GOLF GEAR COSTS MORE THAN VACATIONS

The Priority Problem

Golf spending creates interesting family budget conversations. When equipment costs exceed vacation budgets, priorities require creative justification.

"When you seriously consider canceling the family vacation to buy a new set of irons."

GOLF VS. VACATION ECONOMICS:

- Family vacation: $3,000 "one week of memories"
- New iron set: $2,500 "years of disappointment"
- Golf trip: $2,000 "weekend of excuses"
- Equipment upgrade: $1,500 "months of false hope"

"Trip to the Caribbean or a brand-new set of clubs? Guess which one wins."

The golf gear vs. vacation debate reveals true priorities. Vacations create memories; golf equipment creates opportunities for better excuses.

"The only trip I'm planning this year is to the pro shop."

Family Negotiation Strategies

Golf spending requires diplomatic skills that would impress international negotiators. Creative justification becomes essential.

> *"My family wanted a cruise; I told them my new putter is a cruise toward inner peace."*

FAMILY BUDGET NEGOTIATIONS:

- "These clubs are an investment in my mental health"
- "Equipment upgrades will improve my mood on the course"
- "Better gear means shorter rounds, more family time"
- "This purchase will end my need for future purchases" "biggest lie in golf"

> *"Vacations last two weeks. New equipment lasts months... of frustration, but at least I'll look good."*

The family negotiation process reveals the addictive nature of golf equipment purchasing. Logic rarely wins these discussions.

"Honey, this driver will save money by reducing the number of balls I lose."

VACATION TRUTH:

Golf equipment promises permanent improvement; vacations only promise temporary happiness.

Golf-Centric Vacation Planning

"Honey, I found the perfect resort: beach, spa, kids' club... and totally by chance, 36 championship holes"

"We're not going to Scotland for the whisky... It's the legendary courses, obviously"

"Sure, Paris is nice, but do they have a par-5 next to the Eiffel Tower?"

"This hotel is perfect: free breakfast, infinity pool, and look—a PGA course right next door"

"The difference between a regular tourist and a golfer: one looks for museums, the other looks for tee times"

THE PRO SHOP TRAP

Impulse Buying Psychology

Pro shops are designed to separate golfers from their money through strategic placement of "essential" items and "limited-time" offers that happen to coincide with every visit.

 "PRO SHOPS: *where logic goes to die and credit cards go to max out."*

PRO SHOP MARKETING GENIUS:

- "Tournament-used" equipment "used by someone who can actually play"
- "Limited edition" clubs "limited to several thousand units"
- "Professional-grade" accessories "for amateur-grade golfers"
- "Sale" prices "marked up then marked down"

"I went in for tees and came out with a complete bag makeover."

Pro shops understand that frustrated golfers are vulnerable golfers, and vulnerable golfers make expensive purchasing decisions.

> *"The pro shop knows exactly when you've had a bad round—that's when the 'new arrival' display catches your eye."*

The Demo Day Deception

Demo days promise to help you find the "perfect" equipment through scientific testing. What they actually do is create new desires for equipment you didn't know you "needed."

> *"Demo day: where you discover your current clubs are apparently obsolete."*

DEMO DAY REALITY:

- Hit five perfect shots with the demo club
- Immediately forget the 20 terrible shots with your current club
- Convince yourself the demo club is the missing piece

- Purchase decision made based on limited, ideal conditions

"Demo days turn satisfied golfers
into dissatisfied customers."

The demo day deception relies on the golfer's ability to rationalize that good shots come from equipment rather than occasional good swings.

"I hit one good shot with the demo driver and
suddenly my entire bag needed upgrading."

PRO SHOP TRUTH:
They don't sell equipment—they sell hope in
equipment-shaped packages.

Pro Shop Spending Behaviors

"Entered for ball markers, left with a new hybrid and buyer's remorse"

"The pro shop sale sign is the most dangerous hazard on any golf course"

"Demo clubs perform better than purchased clubs—it's basic golf economics"

"I have more golf equipment than the pro shop back-room inventory"

"My pro shop loyalty card should come with financial counseling services"

THE EQUIPMENT JUSTIFICATION GAME

Creative Budgeting

Golf equipment purchases require creative accounting that would challenge forensic auditors. Every purchase needs *a* justification that sounds reasonable to non-golfers.

"These aren't clubs—they're tools for stress management."

EQUIPMENT JUSTIFICATION STRATEGIES:

- Health investment "walking exercise equipment"
- Professional development "business networking tools"

- Educational expense "learning new skills"

- Safety equipment "protection from poor shots"

• • •

"I'm not buying golf clubs; I'm investing in precision-engineered stress relief devices."

• • •

The equipment justification game becomes increasingly creative as purchases become increasingly expensive.

• • •

"This putter isn't a purchase—it's a consultation fee for a putting specialist."

The False Economy Trap

Golf equipment purchases often use "savings" logic that defies mathematical scrutiny. Every discount becomes an opportunity to spend more money while claiming to save money.

"I saved $200 by buying the $800 driver instead of the $1,000 driver."

FALSE ECONOMY EXAMPLES:

- "Buy two, get one free" "need for zero, bought three"
- "Last year's model" "still more expensive than sensible"
- "Professional discount" "professional prices for amateur abilities"
- "Bundle deal" "needed driver, got complete set"

"Golf mathematics: spending $500 to save $100 makes perfect sense."

The false economy trap convinces golfers that spending money is actually a form of saving money, a concept that exists only in golf retail.

"I'm not spending money on golf equipment— I'm collecting vintage investments."

ECONOMIC TRUTH:

Golf accounting operates in a parallel universe where spending equals saving.

CHAPTER 3 TRUTH BOMB

Golf equipment spending is an addiction disguised as optimization. The industry has perfected the art of selling hope to frustrated golfers, and frustrated golfers have perfected the art of buying it.

Your expensive driver won't fix your slice. Your custom-fitted irons won't improve your ball-striking. Your premium putter won't eliminate three-putts. But they will make you look like someone who should be able to do all those things.

The cruel truth is that golf improvement comes from practice, lessons, and time—none of which can be purchased at the pro shop. But equipment purchases are immediate, while improvement is delayed, so we keep buying the immediate satisfaction instead of investing in the delayed gratification.

Golf equipment promises transformation but delivers only the appearance of an upgrade. The real transformation happens between your ears, not in your golf bag.

But until that realization hits, enjoy looking like a million bucks while playing like loose change. At least your disasters will be well-equipped.

"In golf, you can't buy a better swing, but you can definitely buy a more expensive way to swing badly."

Next up: Quick comebacks for when your expensive equipment fails to live up to its expensive promises...

WHEN ROBOTS
TRY TO FIX YOUR GAME

AI EQUIPMENT RECOMMENDATIONS

Golfer: "What driver should I buy?"
AI: "One that comes with a built-in GPS tracker and an apology letter to whoever finds your ball."

. . .

Golfer: "My putter isn't working. Upgrade recommendations?"
ChatGPT: "Have you tried turning it off and on again? Oh wait, that's for computers. Your putting is beyond technological   assistance."

. . .

Golfer: "Which golf ball gives the most distance?"
ChatGPT: "Any ball will give you maximum distance if you hit it with a tennis racket instead of a golf club."

. . .

Golfer: "Should I get fitted for clubs?"
ChatGPT: "Yes, get fitted... for a different sport."

· · ·

Golfer: "What's the best AI golf app?"
ChatGPT: "The calculator... it's the only one that can handle your real score."

GOLF SWING ANALYSIS GONE WRONG

Golfer: "Analyze my swing and tell me what's wrong."
ChatGPT: "Error 404: Swing not found. Please try again with actual golf technique."

· · ·

Golfer: "I keep hitting it fat. What should I adjust?"
ChatGPT: "Your expectations. Also, maybe aim for the ball instead of the ground."

· · ·

Golfer: "My swing plane is inconsistent. Help!"
ChatGPT: "I've analyzed your swing data... You have 47 different swing planes. Pick one and stick with it."

· · ·

Golfer: "Can you predict where my ball will land?"

ChatGPT: "My algorithms suggest: somewhere between here and the International Space Station."

· · ·

A golfer uploaded a swing video for AI analysis. The AI responded: "I've seen this swing before... in a medical textbook about joint injuries."

CHAPTER 4:
WHAT WE ACTUALLY SAY VS. WHAT WE MEAN

THE REAL CONVERSATIONS EVERY GOLFER HAS

Golf is the only sport where you spend more time explaining your shots than actually hitting them. We all have that internal dialogue running constantly: what we're thinking, what we say out loud, and what we really mean.

This chapter is about the conversations every golfer has—with themselves, their playing partners, and anyone unfortunate enough to ask about their round.

> *"How'd you play today?" "Not bad... if you don't count the actual golf."*

GOLF TRUTH:

We all speak fluent golf lie, even to ourselves.

WHAT WE THINK VS. WHAT WE SAY

Think: *"I have no idea where that ball went"*

Say: *"Must have gotten a bad kick"*

. . .

Think: *"I can't putt to save my life"*

Say: *"These greens are really tough today"*

$$\cdots$$

Think: *"I'm terrible at this game"*

Say: *"I'm just working through some swing changes"*

$$\cdots$$

TALKING TO YOURSELF

THE INTERNAL GOLF MONOLOGUE

The Pre-Shot Pep Talk

Every golfer has that conversation with themselves before every shot. It starts optimistic and gets increasingly desperate as the round progresses.

"Okay, this one's going straight down the middle." "Just like the range. Smooth and easy." "Don't think about the water. Definitely don't think about the water." "Why am I thinking about the water?"

FIRST HOLE INTERNAL DIALOGUE:

- "Today's the day I break 80"
- "Perfect conditions, perfect mindset"

- "I can feel this is going to be different"

BY THE 8TH HOLE:

- "Okay, let's just try to break 90"
- "One good hole, that's all I need"
- "Why do I do this to myself?"

BY THE 16TH HOLE:

- "Just don't lose any more balls"
- "Please let this nightmare end"
- "I'm taking up bowling"

> *"The optimism at the first tee never survives contact with actual golf."*

INTERNAL TRUTH:
Your brain lies to you more than your playing partners do.

Post-Shot Self-Negotiation

After every bad shot, there's an immediate internal negotiation about what just happened and whose fault it was.

"That wasn't my swing, that was...
atmospheric interference."

THE FIVE STAGES OF BAD SHOT GRIEF:

1. **Denial:** "That can't be where my ball went"

2. **Anger:** "This stupid club is broken"

3. **Bargaining:** "If I find this ball, I'll practice more"

4. **Depression:** "I'll never be good at this game"

5. **Acceptance:** "Well, that's golf"

"I go through all five stages between
impact and ball landing."

The internal negotiation always concludes with some version of "that wasn't representative of my real ability." Even when it absolutely was.

> *"That shot was an outlier. I'm much better than that... usually... sometimes... in my dreams."*

Self-Talk Reality Check

"Come on, focus!" "after already missing the shot"

"Just like practice!" "nothing like practice"

"Stay positive!" "while clearly frustrated"

"This is supposed to be fun!" "narrator: it was not fun"

"One shot at a time!" "thinking about the previous five bad shots"

TALKING TO PLAYING PARTNERS

THE ART OF MUTUAL DECEPTION

The Compliment Exchange System

Golf partners engage in a complex system of mutual ego protection through strategic compliments and selective memory.

"Nice shot!" "It went 20 yards further than mine, so it's automatically good"

STANDARD GOLF PARTNER EXCHANGES:

- "Good swing" "after any shot that makes contact"
- "Unlucky bounce" "after any shot that finds trouble"
- "You're due for a good one" "after the 6th consecutive bad shot"
- "That's golf" "universal response to any disaster"

"We compliment each other's mediocrity like it's excellence."

The compliment system works because everyone understands that golf partners are really just validating each other's continued participation in an impossible game.

"Your bad shot makes my bad shot feel less bad."

The Scorecard Diplomacy

Keeping score with friends requires diplomatic skills that would impress international negotiators. Everyone knows everyone else is being... generous.

"What'd you have on that hole?" "Seven... well, maybe eight if you count the whiff." "Let's call it seven. That tree kick was unlucky."

SCORECARD NEGOTIATION TACTICS:

- The "gimme" putt from increasingly long distances
- The "foot wedge" for better lies
- The "breakfast ball" on every tee
- The "do-over" for any shot witnessed by someone coughing

"Golf scoring: where friendship is more important than mathematics."

PARTNER TRUTH:

We're all conspirators in each other's golf fantasy.

Weather Discussion Strategy

Weather becomes the universal scapegoat that allows everyone to blame external factors simultaneously.

"This wind is brutal today" really means *"there is no wind,"* and *"Yeah, totally unpredictable"* really means *"We're agreeing to shared delusion."*

WEATHER CONVERSATION PATTERNS:

- Too windy "never just right"
- Too hot/cold "always extreme"
- Greens too fast/slow "never proper speed"
- Course too wet/dry "impossible conditions"

"If weather conditions were ever perfect, we'd have no one to blame but ourselves."

The weather discussion allows the entire group to participate in collective excuse-making without anyone having to take individual responsibility.

"We're not playing badly, we're all victims of the same meteorological conspiracy."

Universal Weather Complaints

"This is definitely not what they forecasted"

"The weather app said sunny with no wind"

"These conditions are unplayable for anyone"

"Even the pros would struggle in this"

"Mother Nature clearly doesn't want us to play golf today"

EXPLAINING YOUR ROUND TO NON-GOLFERS

The Spouse Conversation

Coming home after a bad round requires careful translation of golf disasters into language that won't result in equipment budget restrictions.

Spouse: *"How was golf?"* **You:** *"Challenging. Very educational."* **Translation:** *"I lost six balls and my dignity."*

WHAT YOU SAY VS. WHAT HAPPENED:

- "Worked on course management" = Got lost looking for balls

- "Focused on short game" = Couldn't reach greens in regulation

- "Beautiful day to be outside" = Only good part of the round

- "Good exercise" = Walked five miles looking for balls

"I describe golf rounds like a politician describes policy failures—lots of learning opportunities."

The Monday Morning Office Report

Office golf conversations require strategic editing to maintain professional credibility while acknowledging the weekend's reality.

Colleague: "How was your weekend round?" **You:** "Shot my handicap... from the forward tees... with mulligans."

Office Golf Translation Guide:

- "Played well" = Didn't embarrass myself completely

- "Course was in great shape" = My shots were in terrible   shape

- "Tough conditions" = I made easy shots difficult

- "Good group" = They didn't mock my swing openly

> *"Office golf stories are 30% truth, 70%*
> *optimistic interpretation."*

PROFESSIONAL TRUTH:

Your golf reputation at work is based entirely on
storytelling ability.

Office Golf Conversations

"Yeah, I'm really working on my short game" "after three-putting six greens"

"Just need to get more consistent" "consistently bad doesn't count"

"The course played really long today" "my shots played really short"

"Had a few unlucky breaks" "had a few dozen unlucky swings"

"Starting to put it all together" "falling apart in new and creative ways"

THE PRO SHOP CONFESSION

Equipment Consultation Theater

Pro shop conversations involve admitting your problems to someone whose job is to sell you solutions, creating a unique form of therapeutic retail.

Pro Shop Guy: "How can I help you?" **You:** "I need something that will help my slice... and my hook... and my chunks... and my skulls."

Pro Shop Translation:

- "Looking for more forgiveness" = I need miracles
- "Want to improve my consistency" = I'm wildly inconsistent
- "Seeking better feel" = I can't feel anything anymore
- "Need more confidence" = Please sell me some self-esteem

"Pro shop conversations are therapy sessions disguised as sales consultations."

The Lesson Booking Humility

Booking a golf lesson requires admitting that, despite years of playing and thousands of dollars in equipment, you still need help with basics.

Golf Pro: "What would you like to work on?" **You:** "Everything. Literally everything. Can we start with making contact?"

LESSON BOOKING HONESTY LEVELS:

- Level 1: "Just need a tune-up"
- Level 2: "Working through some swing issues"
- Level 3: "Need fundamental help"
- Level 4: "Please teach me how to play golf"
- Level 5: "Is it too late to take up tennis?"

"Golf lessons are where honesty meets humility in expensive increments."

LESSON TRUTH:

Admitting you need help costs $100 per hour.

TEACHING YOUR KIDS GOLF

PASSING DOWN THE LANGUAGE OF DENIAL

Introducing children to golf requires teaching them two separate skill sets: how to swing a club and how to explain why the ball didn't go where intended. The excuse education often proves more valuable than swing instruction.

"Dad, why didn't your ball go in the hole?"
"Well, son, that putt was affected by... uh...
underground magnetic fields."

KID GOLF TRANSLATION CHALLENGES:

- Explaining why expensive equipment doesn't guarantee success
- Teaching patience when you display none
- Demonstrating sportsmanship while arguing with inanimate objects

- Showing them "proper" form while consistently demonstrating improper results

>  **"TEACHING KIDS GOLF:**
>
> *passing down generations of creative accountability avoidance."*

Children have an uncomfortable habit of asking direct questions that expose the logical flaws in adult golf reasoning.

> "Daddy, if the wind moved your ball, why didn't it move mine?" "Because... uh... you're shorter, so the wind goes over your head."
>
> ———⚑———

Junior Excuse Development

Kids learn golf excuses faster than golf swings because the excuses make more immediate sense than the actual technique.

CHILD EXCUSE EVOLUTION:

- Age 6: "The ball didn't listen to me"
- Age 8: "My club is broken"
- Age 10: "That wasn't fair"
- Age 12: "The course is too hard"

- Age 14: "This is stupid" "peak honesty phase"

> *"Children's golf excuses start honest and gradually become sophisticated lies like their parents'."*

Parent-Child Golf Conversations

"Why do you throw your club, Dad?" "I'm not throwing it, I'm... repositioning it dynamically."

"Why did you say those words?" "Those are special golf words for when physics stops working."

"Are you winning?" "Golf isn't about winning, it's about... character development."

"Can we go home now?" "Just 9 more holes of character development, sweetie."

GOLFING WITH YOUR BOSS:

CORPORATE EXCUSE DIPLOMACY

Playing golf with your boss creates a complex diplomatic situation where you must balance competitive instincts with career advancement considerations. The conversations become exercises in corporate politics disguised as sports commentary.

"Great shot, sir! That slice really showed strategic course management."

BOSS GOLF CONVERSATION RULES:

- Never outdrive your boss "too obvious"

- Never outscore your boss "career-limiting"

- Always compliment their equipment choices

- Blame their bad shots on external factors more elaborate than your own

 "PLAYING GOLF WITH YOUR BOSS: *where honest feedback becomes a résumé risk."*

The Promotion Putt Dilemma

The most dangerous moment in corporate golf occurs when your boss faces a putt that could determine their mood for the next quarter's performance reviews.

"That's good, boss!" "from 8 feet away" "No, no, I'll putt it." "career anxiety intensifies" "Great read! That break was impossible to see." "regardless of outcome"

CORPORATE GOLF EXCUSE HIERARCHY:

- Your bad shots: Personal responsibility and learning opportunities

- Boss's bad shots: Unfair course conditions and equipment   malfunctions

- Your good shots: Lucky breaks and favorable conditions

- Boss's good shots: Superior technique and strategic thinking

 "CORPORATE GOLF: *where the scorecard matters less than the performance review."*

Office Golf Survival Guide

"Your drive went further than expected, boss." "It went 150 yards"

"These greens are definitely not rolling true today." "After boss three-putts"

"You're really working that fade to your advantage." "Slice management"

"That's exactly where I would have aimed it." "In the water   hazard"

"This course doesn't do justice to your real ability." "Universal   safe   response"

GOLF WIDOW CONVERSATIONS

EXPLAINING THE INEXPLICABLE

Golf widows "spouses of obsessed golfers" develop a unique vocabulary for discussing their partners' mysterious hobby that consumes weekends, budgets, and emotional stability. These conversations happen in kitchens, offices, and anywhere golf widows gather for support.

> *"How was Jim's golf today?" "He shot his weight... if he weighed 250 pounds."*

GOLF WIDOW SUPPORT GROUP TOPICS:

- Translation of golf terminology into actual English
- Budget impact analysis of "essential" equipment purchases
- Decoding emotional states based on golf performance
- Understanding why grown men can be defeated by tiny balls

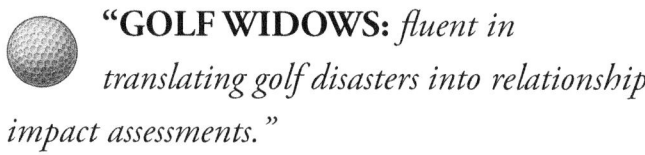

"GOLF WIDOWS: *fluent in translating golf disasters into relationship impact assessments."*

Decoding Golf Mood Reports

Golf widows become expert meteorologists, predicting household weather patterns based on golf performance reports received via text during rounds.

TEXT MESSAGE TRANSLATION GUIDE:

- "Playing great!" = Currently 2 over par "honeymoon period"

- "Tough conditions" = Currently 8 over par "reality setting in"

- "Long day" = Currently 15 over par "damage control mode"

- "See you later" = Lost count, seeking alcohol therapy

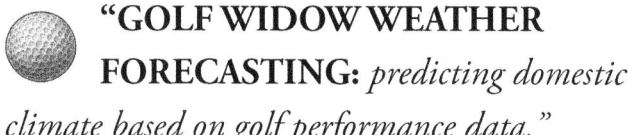

"GOLF WIDOW WEATHER FORECASTING: *predicting domestic climate based on golf performance data."*

The Equipment Justification Hearing

Golf widows regularly preside over informal budget hearings where new equipment purchases must be justified using creative accounting that would challenge forensic auditors.

"Honey, this driver will actually save us money." "How does a $600 club save money?" "Well, it'll reduce the number of balls I lose, and those add up." "You lost 12 balls last weekend with your old driver." "Exactly! This one will cut that in half."

STANDARD EQUIPMENT JUSTIFICATION DEFENSES:

- Investment in mental health and stress management

- Professional development for business networking

- Exercise equipment for cardiovascular health

- Educational tools for learning patience and humility

> **"GOLF WIDOWS:** *unpaid accountants specializing in recreational equipment depreciation analysis."*

Golf Widow Budget Negotiations

"It's not a purchase, it's a long-term investment in my happiness."

"This lesson package will save money by reducing future equipment needs."

"Golf trips are actually more economical than regular vacations."

"Pro shop sales are basically free money if you think about it correctly."

"I'm not spending money on golf, I'm investing in relationship preservation through stress relief."

THE 19TH HOLE STORYTELLING

Selective Memory Championship

The 19th hole is where golf rounds are reimagined through the lens of selective memory and creative storytelling. Bad shots disappear, good shots multiply, and near-misses become moral victories.

> **"*I was putting really well today... if you don't count the three-putts.*"**

19TH HOLE STORY ENHANCEMENT:

- "Had several birdie chances" "missed 15-foot putts"
- "Really struck it well" "made solid contact twice"

- "Could have been a great round" "if 12 shots had been different"

- "Everything was just a little off" "everything was way off"

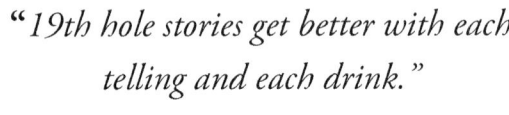

> *"19th hole stories get better with each telling and each drink."*

The Group Therapy Session

Golf buddies serve as unpaid therapists, listening to each other's round analysis with the understanding that everyone gets equal time to complain.

> *"I know exactly what I'm doing wrong, I just can't stop doing it."*

STANDARD 19TH HOLE THERAPY:

- Swing analysis by people who can't swing

- Equipment recommendations from fellow strugglers

- Course management advice from people who can't manage their games

- Psychological support from equally frustrated golfers

"We're all blind leading the blind, but at least we're walking together."

The 19th hole therapy session allows everyone to verbally process their round while drinking away the memory of what actually happened.

"Golf therapy: where everyone's an expert on everyone else's problems."

19TH HOLE TRUTH:

The drinks get better as the golf gets worse.

Classic 19th Hole onversations

"I was one putt away from shooting my age" "if my age were 95"

"Everything was pin high today" "20 feet past the pin is still pin high"

"Just couldn't get anything to drop" "because I wasn't hitting   greens"

"The course was playing really tough" "I was playing really bad"

"I'll get 'em next time" "narrator: he would not get them next time"

CHAPTER 4 TRUTH BOMB

Golf conversations are elaborate defense mechanisms designed to protect our egos from the harsh reality of our actual performance. We develop sophisticated translation systems to convert disasters into learning experiences, failures into near-successes, and embarrassment into entertainment.

The conversations we have about golf—with ourselves, our partners, our families, and anyone who'll listen—are really negotiations with reality. We're constantly trying to reconcile our golf aspirations with our golf abilities, and language becomes the tool we use to bridge that impossible gap.

Everyone speaks fluent golf excuse because everyone needs the same psychological protection from the same impossible game. We're all in this together, translating our shared struggles into digestible stories that allow us to keep coming back for more.

The real skill in golf isn't hitting better shots—it's developing better ways to explain why the shots weren't better. And in that skill, we're all scratch players.

Golf conversations aren't about what happened—they're about how we choose to remember what happened."

Next up: Embracing the beautiful absurdity that makes all these conversations necessary...

ONE-LINER JOKES FOR EVERY HOLE

YOUR ROUND-BY-ROUND COMEDY ARSENAL

PERFECT FOR KEEPING THE MOOD LIGHT FROM TEE TO GREEN

Hole 1: The Optimistic Start

"First hole optimism: where dreams go to die in the most beautiful setting possible."

Usage: Perfect for the opening tee shot, regardless of outcome. Sets expectations appropriately low while maintaining hope.

· · ·

Hole 2: Reality Check

"Second hole reality: apparently my practice swing was just showing off."

Usage: When your first-hole performance doesn't carry over. Acknowledges that consistency is a myth.

· · ·

Hole 3: Pattern Recognition

"Three holes in: I've officially established a pattern of creative disappointment."

Usage: When you realize your round is developing a theme. Turns statistical analysis into comedy.

· · ·

Hole 4: Equipment Evaluation

"Hole four assessment: my clubs are having trust issues with my swing."

Usage: When equipment performance becomes questionable. Suggests relationship counseling for you and your gear.

· · ·

Hole 5: Weather Consultation

"Fifth hole meteorology: I'm now personally monitoring atmospheric
conditions for ball-flight interference."

Usage: When environmental factors become your primary concern. Positions you as a weather expert.

· · ·

Hole 6: Wildlife Relations

"Halfway point wildlife report: the local squirrel union has definitely
organized against our group."

Usage: When animal interference reaches conspiracy levels. Acknowledges coordinated natural opposition.

· · ·

Hole 7: Strategic Reassessment

"Seven holes down: time to lower expectations and raise entertainment value."

Usage: Mid-round pivot from scoring to enjoying. Officially changes your round's primary objective.

• • •

Hole 8: Technical Analysis

"Hole eight technical review: my swing is experiencing software compatibility issues."

Usage: When mechanical problems persist. Suggests your swing needs a system update or reboot.

• • •

Hole 9: Front Nine Summary

"Front nine complete: I've successfully tested every possible way to not hit a golf ball straight."

Usage: Turn poor performance into comprehensive research. You're not struggling—you're being thorough.

• • •

Hole 10: Fresh Start Philosophy

"Back nine begins: new holes, same chaos, slightly less optimism."

Usage: Acknowledges that the back nine is a fresh opportunity with realistic expectations based on recent evidence.

· · ·

Hole 11: Psychological Evaluation

"Eleven holes in: my golf ball has officially developed separation anxiety from the fairway."

Usage: When wayward shots become a consistent theme. Suggests psychological issues with your equipment.

· · ·

Hole 12: Course Relations

"Hole twelve diplomacy: apparently I'm in ongoing peace negotiations with this golf course."

Usage: When you and the course seem to be in conflict. Positions golf as international relations.

. . .

Hole 13: Superstition Activation

"Lucky thirteen: where superstition meets statistical probability and both lose."

Usage: Perfect for the traditionally unlucky hole number. Acknowledges that both luck and logic have abandoned you.

. . .

Hole 14: Energy Management

"Fourteen holes deep: I'm conserving energy for the walk back to the clubhouse."

Usage: When fatigue sets in and priorities shift. Suggests strategic energy allocation for post-round activities.

. . .

Hole 15: Mathematical Analysis

"Hole fifteen calculation: my scorecard now requires scientific notation."

Usage: When numbers get uncomfortably large. Turns scoring embarrassment into mathematical comedy.

. . .

Hole 16: Equipment Loyalty Assessment

"Sixteen holes in: my clubs and I are officially in couples therapy."

Usage: When the relationship with your equipment reaches a crisis point. Suggests professional intervention needed.

. . .

Hole 17: Pressure Management

"Seventeen down: the only pressure I feel now is atmospheric, and it's working against me."

Usage: When traditional golf pressure is replaced by environmental conspiracy theories. Meteorology becomes your primary concern.

. . .

Hole 18: Final Assessment

"Eighteenth hole philosophy: I came, I saw, I donated
generously
to the golf ball wildlife fund."

Usage: Final hole summary that frames ball loss as
charitable giving.
Ends the round on a philanthropic note.

BONUS EMERGENCY ONE-LINERS

For Any Hole Disaster:

- "That shot was performance art—abstract and open to interpretation."

- "I'm not playing golf badly, I'm redefining what golf can be."

- "My ball is clearly majoring in geography with a minor in adventure studies."

. . .

For Particularly Spectacular Failures:

- "That shot just applied for its own zip code."

- "I think my ball is writing its memoirs about this round."

- "My golf game is like jazz—it's all about the improvisation."

PERFORMANCE TIP:

Timing is everything. Deliver these lines immediately after the shot while the disaster is fresh. Hesitation kills comedy.

GROUP DYNAMIC:

These work best when your playing partners are in on the joke. Lead with self-deprecation to invite shared laughter rather than sympathy.

ESCALATION STRATEGY:

Start subtle and get progressively more absurd as the round continues. By hole 18, you should be blaming quantum physics.

CHAPTER 5:
EMBRACING GOLF'S BEAUTIFUL ABSURDITY

Let's be honest about what golf really is: a game where grown adults dress like 1920s country club members, whisper like they're in a library, and spend four hours trying to put a tiny ball into holes that are deliberately placed in the most inconvenient locations possible.

We chase this ball around manicured landscapes using implements that would be considered medieval torture devices in any other context, all while pretending this makes perfect sense.

"Golf: the only sport where you dress like a butler and play like a disaster."

"We're basically playing 18 holes of 'the floor is lava' with expensive sticks."

And you know what? It's absolutely magnificent.

> *"Golf is perfectly designed to be imperfectly played by imperfect people with imperfect equipment."*
>
>

GOLF TRUTH:

The more ridiculous golf becomes, the more addictive it gets.

Why Golf Is Beautifully Absurd

- "It's the only game where you can lose your ball, your temper, and your dignity simultaneously"

- "We pay money to make ourselves angry in beautiful places"

- "The rules were written by people who clearly don't want anyone to have fun"

- "Success is measured by how few times you hit the ball"

- "The smaller the target, the more expensive the equipment required to miss it"

THE RULEBOOK

A MASTERPIECE OF BUREAUCRATIC COMEDY

Rules That Sound Made Up "But Aren't"

Golf's official rulebook reads like it was written by a committee of lawyers, philosophers, and people who really enjoy making simple things complicated.

"THE GOLF RULEBOOK: *200 pages of reasons why your shot doesn't count."*

RULE 14.3

You can't use artificial devices to help with your game, except for the dozens that are specifically allowed, unless they're used in ways that aren't allowed, which is determined by people who meet annually to argue about what constitutes "assistance."

 GOLF RULES: *making rocket science look straightforward since 1744."*

This rule basically says you can't use technology to help your golf game, except for the $500 rangefinders, GPS watches, launch monitors, and smart putters that everyone uses.

"I can't use a device to read putts, but I can use a device that measures wind speed, elevation, and atmospheric pressure."

RULE 16.1

When your ball is on the putting green, you can mark it, clean it, and replace it, but only after following a ritual that would make a medieval ceremony look casual.

"Putting green etiquette requires more precision than NASA mission protocols."

You have to put your ball back where it "would have been" if things that happened hadn't happened. It's quantum physics disguised as recreational activity.

"Golf is the only sport where you play with invisible time travel."

. . .

RULE PHILOSOPHY: *If it makes sense, it's probably not a golf rule.*

The Penalty System: Golf's Criminal Justice Program

Golf is the only sport where you're punished for equipment failure. If your ball goes somewhere you didn't intend, you don't just play from the bad location—you also add penalty strokes for your ball's poor life choices.

"Golf literally fines you for your equipment's refusal to cooperate."

PENALTY LOGIC

- Ball goes in water: Penalty stroke "punishment for trusting aerodynamics"

- Ball goes out of bounds: Penalty stroke "punishment for optimistic target selection"

- Ball moves on green: Penalty stroke "punishment for natural phenomena"

- Ball hits another ball: Penalty stroke "punishment for traffic accidents"

"The penalty system treats golf balls like they have free will and moral responsibility."

This would be like getting a speeding ticket because your car decided to accelerate without permission, or being charged with assault because your handshake was too firm.

*"Golf penalties assume your equipment is
capable of making independent decisions."*

Golf is the only sport where inanimate objects are held legally accountable for their actions.

*"My ball has a worse criminal
record than most humans."*

Golf Rule Translation Guide

"You may take relief" = *"This will somehow make things worse"*

"Play it as it lies" = *"Good luck with that impossible shot"*

"Nearest point of relief" = *"Congratulations, you found a worse lie"*

"Ground under repair" = *"This area is broken, but so is everywhere else"*

"Casual water" = *"This puddle has legal standing in golf court"*

. . .

FASHION POLICE

WHEN ATHLETIC WEAR BECOMES COSTUME PARTY

The Tradition of Tactical Plaid

Golf is the only sport where plaid pants are not just acceptable but encouraged. Golfers routinely wear color combinations that would get them escorted from any other public venue.

> *"Golf fashion: where loud pants are a statement and quiet pants are a missed opportunity."*

The golf wardrobe exists in its own fashion dimension where bright pink shirts pair with lime green pants, and everyone pretends this is normal.

> *"I dress like a 1970s game show host, and somehow that qualifies as 'athletic wear.'"*

GOLF FASHION RULES:

- If it doesn't hurt to look at, it's not golf attire

- Color coordination is for amateurs

- The louder the pattern, the better the golfer "supposedly"

- Matching is discouraged as a sign of taking things too seriously

"My outfit generates more comments than my golf swing."

The fashion rules suggest that visual disruption somehow improves athletic performance, like camouflage for golf balls.

"I'm dressed to distract—myself and everyone else."

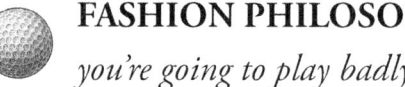 **FASHION PHILOSOPHY**: *If you're going to play badly, at least look interesting while doing it.*

The Collar Requirement Conspiracy

Golf demands shirts with collars because apparently your neck needs a formal introduction to the golf course. A T-shirt is considered inappropriate for chasing a ball around a field.

> *"Collars: because golf balls can apparently tell the difference between formal and casual neckwear."*

COLLAR LOGIC

- T-shirts lack respect for the game "according to who?"

- Polo shirts demonstrate proper golf appreciation "how?"

- Tank tops are banned "discrimination against shoulders"

- Collars somehow improve swing mechanics "citation needed"

> *"My shirt has more class requirements than some restaurants."*

The collar conspiracy extends to clubhouse dining, where the same shirt that's acceptable for hitting balls becomes unacceptable for eating sandwiches.

"Apparently my collar loses its magical golf powers when I enter the restaurant."

Golf is the only sport where clothing has jurisdiction-specific approval ratings.

"My polo shirt has a better dress code understanding than I do."

Golf Fashion Excuses

"My outfit is so loud, it should come with a noise ordinance   violation"

"I'm dressed like a walking rainbow having an identity crisis"

"This shirt was visible from space, which helped my playing partners find me in the rough"

"My pants are loud enough to wake up my golf game—unfortunately, nothing happened"

"I look like a golf pro shop exploded on me"

COURSE DESIGN

LANDSCAPE ARCHITECTURE BY SADISTS

The Strategic Placement of Misery

Golf course designers are landscape architects with psychology degrees and apparent grudges against human happiness. They study ball flight patterns specifically to identify where balls want to go, then make those areas uninhabitable.

> *"Course designers: making beautiful places as frustrating as possible to navigate."*

DESIGN PHILOSOPHY

- If it's pleasant, make it a hazard
- If it's logical, move it somewhere illogical
- If it looks easy, add hidden complications
- If it seems fair, increase the difficulty

> *"Golf course design: where beauty meets malice
> in perfect harmony."*

WATER HAZARD PLACEMENT: Designers dig holes in perfectly good land, fill them with water, and position them with magnetic precision where golf balls naturally want to land.

> **"WATER HAZARDS:** *nature's way of saying
> 'you can't have nice things.'"*

SAND BUNKER STRATEGY: Replace perfectly good grass with sand, creating artificial beaches in landlocked locations specifically designed to trap golf balls.

> *"Bunkers: beaches without the relaxation
> or the ocean views."*

TREE PRESERVATION PROGRAM:

Keep vegetation exactly where it will interfere with golf shots while removing it from areas where it might actually help.

 "TREES: *the only audience that never applauds but always participates."*

DESIGN TRUTH:

Golf courses are basically obstacle courses disguised as parks.

Pin Placement: Strategic Torture

Every morning, course maintenance crews ask themselves: "Where can we put today's pins to maximize human suffering?" These placement specialists have turned flag positioning into psychological warfare.

"Pin placement committees clearly moonlight as medieval torture consultants."

DAILY PIN PLACEMENT GOALS:

- Behind bunkers "approach shot intimidation"
- On slopes "gravity-defying putt requirements"
- Near water "psychological warfare tactics"
- In corners "geometric impossibility challenges"

> *"Today's pins are located in dimensions where normal physics don't apply."*

TYPICAL PIN PLACEMENT MEETING: "Where should we put the pin on 12?" "How about three inches left of impossible and two feet short of ridiculous?" "Perfect. Make sure it's visible from the tee so they get false hope."

> *"Pin placement: designed by people who've clearly given up on human happiness."*

The most diabolical pins look reasonable from 150 yards but reveal their true evil nature only after you've committed to your approach shot.

> *"That pin placement violates several international treaties on fair play."*

Pin Placement Comedy

"The pin is hidden behind a bunker, like it's in witness protection"

"Today's pin location requires a shot that defies three laws of physics"

"The flag is positioned where only mathematicians and miracle workers can reach it"

"This green was designed by someone who clearly hates golf"

"The pin placement committee meets daily to brainstorm new ways to destroy dreams"

GOLF PSYCHOLOGY

MENTAL GYMNASTICS AS COMPETITIVE SPORT

The Confidence Paradox

Golf demands unshakeable confidence in demonstrably shaky abilities. You must believe you can make every shot while possessing overwhelming statistical evidence that you can't.

"Golf requires faith-based confidence in science-based impossibility."

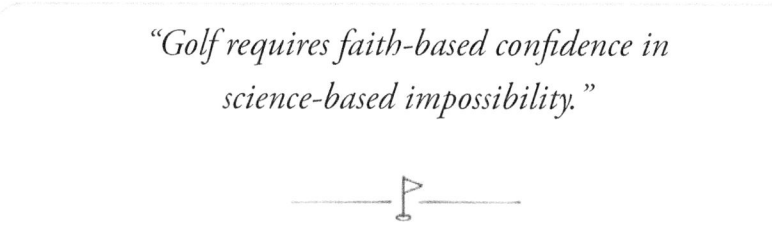

THE CONFIDENCE CHALLENGE:

- Believe in success despite history of failure
- Maintain optimism in the face of mathematical probability
- Stay positive while evidence suggests otherwise
- Trust your swing despite its proven unreliability

"I have to maintain confidence in abilities that exist mostly in theory."

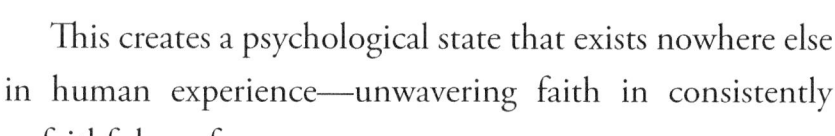

This creates a psychological state that exists nowhere else in human experience—unwavering faith in consistently unfaithful performance.

> *"My self-confidence and my scorecard are*
> *in an abusive relationship."*

Golf confidence is like believing in unicorns while looking at statistical evidence that they don't exist. But you have to believe anyway, or the game becomes impossible instead of just improbable.

 "GOLF PSYCHOLOGY: *maintaining sanity while participating in organized insanity."*

 MENTAL GAME: *Where positive thinking meets negative reality and they argue constantly.*

Memory Management Disorder

Golf requires selective amnesia combined with perfect recall. Remember every detail about successful shots while completely forgetting unsuccessful ones exist.

 "GOLF MEMORY: *HD recording for good shots, complete data corruption for bad ones."*

MEMORY MANAGEMENT REQUIREMENTS:

- Perfect recall of that one good drive from 1997

- Complete amnesia about the slice from five minutes ago

- Detailed analysis of successful techniques

- Strategic forgetting of disasters for confidence preservation

> *"My brain has a very sophisticated filing system—all the good stuff goes in permanent storage, all the bad stuff gets deleted immediately."*

This selective memory system would be considered a psychological disorder in any other context. Imagine accountants who only remembered successful calculations.

"I remember shots that never happened and forget shots that definitely occurred."

• • • • •

Golf memory management requires the cognitive flexibility of a CIA operative and the denial capacity of a reality TV star.

• • • • •

"My golf brain operates like a political campaign—selective facts, creative interpretation, and unwavering optimism despite evidence."

Golf Psychology Quick Hits

"Golf confidence is 90% delusion and 10% hope"

"I have a PhD in positive thinking and a kindergarten-level golf game"

"My mental game is stronger than my actual game, which isn't saying much"

"Golf psychology: where self-help meets self-sabotage"

"I'm mentally tough enough to forget how bad I am at golf"

· · · · ·

THE SOCIAL DYNAMICS

FRIENDSHIP THROUGH SHARED SUFFERING

Bonding Through Mutual Incompetence

Golf creates friendships through collective humiliation. Nothing brings people together like watching each other fail spectacularly at the same ridiculous task.

 "GOLF BUDDIES: *the only people who've seen you cry over a game and didn't judge."*

Golf Friendship Foundations:

- Shared understanding of impossible expectations
- Mutual appreciation for creative excuse-making
- Collective acceptance of equipment betrayal
- Group therapy through recreational activity

"We bond over shared incompetence and mutual encouragement."

Golf relationships are built on the understanding that

everyone struggles with the same fundamental problem: trying to hit a tiny ball with a stick while maintaining dignity.

"Golf friends understand your pain because they're experiencing identical suffering."

These relationships transcend normal social boundaries because they're founded on vulnerability, shared failure, and mutual support through impossible challenges.

"My golf buddies have seen me at my worst and keep inviting me back—that's true friendship."

 GOLF FRIENDSHIP: *Where shared disasters create unbreakable bonds.*

The Handicap System: Mathematical Fiction

Golf's handicap system is pure statistical optimism designed to maintain hope despite overwhelming evidence. It calculates potential ability based on occasional success while ignoring typical performance reality.

 'THE HANDICAP SYSTEM:
mathematical proof that I'm better than I actually am."

HANDICAP CALCULATION LOGIC:

- Takes your best rounds "selective data sampling"
- Ignores your typical rounds "inconvenient truth elimination"
- Projects future performance based on past anomalies "optimistic forecasting"
- Creates mathematical evidence of improvement that doesn't exist "statistical magic"

"My handicap represents the golfer I could theoretically become in an alternate universe."

This system tells you that you're better than you are, using complex calculations to prove that your disasters don't count and your miracles represent your "true" ability.

"The handicap system is like a participation trophy with mathematical credentials."

It's institutionalized optimism that keeps golfers returning despite mounting evidence that improvement is largely theoretical.

"My handicap is based on potential energy, not kinetic reality."

Handicap System Comedy

"My handicap calculation includes shots from dreams I had about golf"

"The math says I'm improving; my scorecard filed a complaint"

"My handicap is more optimistic than my financial advisor"

"I have a statistical golf game that exists only on paper"

EQUIPMENT ARMS RACE

TECHNOLOGY VS. REALITY

The Promise of Instant Improvement

Golf equipment manufacturers have convinced millions that swing flaws can be solved through purchasing decisions. Every year brings new technologies promising to transform incompetence into competence through titanium and graphite.

> *"Equipment manufacturers: selling hope in aerodynamically designed packages."*

THE EQUIPMENT PROMISE:

- New driver will fix your slice "it won't"

- Better irons will improve accuracy "doubtful"

- Advanced putters will solve putting problems "unlikely"

- Premium balls will add distance "for someone else"

"I have NASA-level technology in my bag and stone-age talent in my hands."

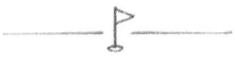

This creates an industry based on selling technological solutions to what are fundamentally human problems.

"Golf equipment evolution: clubs get smarter while golfers stay exactly the same."

The equipment arms race means golfers own gear more sophisticated than their ability to use it effectively.

"My clubs are smarter than I am, but we still can't figure out golf together."

 EQUIPMENT REALITY: *Advanced technology meets basic human limitation and loses every time.*

Customization Obsession

Golf equipment can be fitted with precision that would impress rocket scientists. Clubs are customized for lie angle, loft, shaft flex, and swing weight with scientific accuracy that assumes the golfer has consistent swing characteristics.

> *"My clubs are custom-fitted for a swing*
> *I don't actually possess."*

FITTING PROCESS ABSURDITY:

- Measure swing speed "varies by 20 mph depending on day"

- Calculate optimal loft "assumes consistent contact"

- Determine proper lie angle "presumes repeatable swing plane"

- Select ideal shaft flex "pretends golfers have one swing"

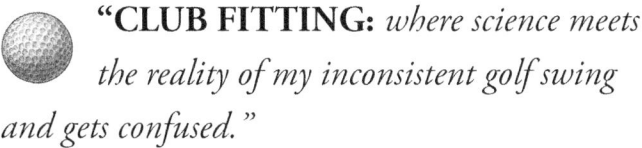

"CLUB FITTING: *where science meets the reality of my inconsistent golf swing and gets confused."*

This precision customization for imprecise performers is beautifully contradictory—like tailoring suits for people who change size randomly.

> *"I have clubs fitted to tolerances tighter than my ability to use them."*

The fitting process assumes golfers are sophisticated biological machines when they're actually chaos generators with golf aspirations.

> *"My swing analysis looks like a seismograph during an earthquake."*

Equipment Philosophy

"I collect golf clubs like some people collect art—expensive and mostly decorative"

"My equipment budget exceeds the GDP of small nations"

"I'm single-handedly keeping the golf industry profitable through optimistic purchasing"

"My clubs cost more than my car and perform about as reliably"

"Technology improves; my golf game remains historically consistent"

WHY GOLF'S ABSURDITY IS PERFECT

The Great Equalizer Effect

Golf's fundamental absurdity serves as the ultimate leveling mechanism. The game is designed to make everyone look foolish regardless of skill level, income, education, or social status.

> **"GOLF:** *where CEOs and construction workers look equally ridiculous."*

GOLF'S EQUALIZING POWERS

- Expensive equipment doesn't guarantee success

- Professional instruction can't overcome physics

- Perfect practice conditions don't transfer to the course

- Social status provides no protection from three-putts

> *"Golf doesn't care about your resume—it only cares about your ability to hit a tiny ball with a stick."*

This forced humility is surprisingly therapeutic. Golf strips away pretense and ego with ruthless efficiency.

> *"Golf taught me that looking foolish isn't actually harmful to my health."*

The humility lesson extends beyond golf. Once you've accepted public incompetence in one area, other life challenges seem manageable.

> *"After golf humiliation, everything else feels like a confidence booster."*

GOLF WISDOM: *Shared absurdity creates genuine human connection.*

The Patience Development Program

Golf operates on geological timescales disguised as recreational activity. Improvement happens so slowly it's nearly imperceptible, requiring patience that challenges modern attention spans.

> *"Golf improvement occurs at the speed of continental drift."*

PATIENCE TRAINING FEATURES:

- Progress measured in decades, not rounds

- Success defined by marginal improvement over vast timeframes

- Gratification delayed indefinitely with occasional false hope

- Expectations managed through realistic disappointment

"I've been working on the same swing flaw since the Clinton administration."

This forced patience development is increasingly valuable in an instant-gratification world.

"Golf teaches you to work toward long-term goals while accepting short-term disasters."

The patience training includes emotional regulation—managing frustration, disappointment, and anger while continuing to function.

"GOLF PATIENCE: *accepting that meaningful change requires more time than most civilizations last."*

TIME PHILOSOPHY: *Golf proves that good things come to those who wait... and wait... and wait.*

GOLF LIFE LESSONS

"Golf teaches humility faster than any other sport or life experience"

• • •

"Patience in golf translates to patience everywhere else— everything seems quick after golf improvement timelines"

• • •

"Golf resilience: if you can bounce back from a quadruple bogey, you can handle anything"

• • •

"GOLF ACCEPTANCE: *learning to control what you can and laugh at what you can't"*

• • •

"GOLF PERSPECTIVE: *after missing a 2-foot putt, work deadlines don't seem so stressful"*

• • •

Universal Absurdity Wisdom

"If you can accept golf's absurdity, you can accept any absurdity"

• • •

"Golf teaches you that some things are inherently ridiculous and that's perfectly fine"

• • •

"Learning to laugh at golf disasters makes every other life problem seem manageable"

• • •

"Golf absurdity is practice for life absurdity—which is everywhere"

• • •

"The ability to find humor in hopeless situations is golf's greatest gift"

CHAPTER 5 TRUTH BOMB

Golf's absurdity isn't a design flaw—it's the entire operating system. The game's fundamental weirdness is what makes it endlessly fascinating, surprisingly addictive, and accidentally perfect as a life training program.

The rules will never make complete sense. The fashion will always be questionable. Course design will remain strategically sadistic. Equipment will continue promising miracles while delivering reality. Your psychology will battle physics and lose consistently.

And that's exactly what makes golf magnificent.

Once you accept that golf is beautifully, perfectly, magnificently absurd, you can stop fighting the absurdity and start appreciating it. The game transforms from a source of frustration into a source of wonder, comedy, and surprisingly deep life lessons.

Golf is designed to be imperfectly played by imperfect people using imperfect equipment under imperfect conditions. This isn't a bug—it's the entire point.

Every golfer eventually realizes the game isn't about getting a ball into holes. It's about learning to find joy, friendship, and personal growth through participation in humanity's most wonderfully ridiculous recreational activity.

"Golf's absurdity is its greatest feature—embrace it, celebrate it, and let it teach you that some of life's best experiences make absolutely no logical sense."

CLASSIC GOLF ONE-LINERS:

TIMELESS JOKES EVERY GOLFER SHOULD KNOW

THE ESSENTIAL COLLECTION OF GOLF COMEDY GOLD

These jokes have survived decades of retelling because they capture universal golf truths

THE FUNDAMENTALS

"Golf is a good walk spoiled." — Mark Twain

. . .

"Golf is the only sport where you can improve
your lie and still tell the truth."

. . .

"I golf in the low 80s. If it's any hotter, I won't play."

. . .

"Golf is like taxes—you drive hard to get to the
green, and then wind up in the hole."

. . .

"The difference between golf and government is that in
golf you can't improve your lie."

. . .

SCORING REALITY

"My handicap? Woods and irons."

. . .

"I don't have a handicap—I'm all handicap."

. . .

"Golf is a game where you yell 'fore,' shoot six,
and write down five."

. . .

"My best score ever? 72. Unfortunately,
that was just the front nine."

• • •

"I shot my age yesterday. I'm 85."

• • •

EQUIPMENT TRUTH

"Golf clubs are the only things that work better when
you're not using them."

• • •

"I have a furniture problem with my golf
clubs—my drives always end up in the living
room... of someone else's house."

• • •

"The only thing worse than a golfer who
can't putt is one who can."

• • •

"My clubs and I have an understanding—they don't
work, and I don't expect them to."

• • •

"I've got the game down to two strokes: the one
I take and the one I have afterward."

• • •

COURSE WISDOM

"Golf is nature's way of teaching you that
perfection is impossible."

• • •

"The trees are 90 percent air, so how come I keep hitting
the 10 percent that's wood?"

• • •

"Water hazards are like magnets—they only attract the
balls you can't afford to lose."

• • •

"The closer you get to the green, the
smaller the target becomes."

• • •

"Every golf course has at least one impossible hole
designed by a committee that hates golfers."

• • •

PLAYING PARTNERS

"Golf is the only game where the worst player gets the
most strokes."

• • •

"Never play golf with a man named after a city."

• • •

"The most important shot in golf is the next one."

• • •

"Golf partners are like mushrooms—keep them in
the dark and feed them manure."

• • •

"Playing golf with your spouse is like being audited—
someone's always keeping score."

• • •

PRACTICE PHILOSOPHY

"Golf is 90 percent mental and 10 percent mental."

• • •

"Practice makes perfect, but nobody's perfect,
so why practice?"

• • •

"The harder I practice, the luckier I get... at other sports."

• • •

"Range time is like church—you feel better for going, but
it doesn't actually improve your behavior."

• • •

"I practice my swing everywhere except on the golf course,
where it mysteriously stops working."

• • •

WEATHER EXCUSES

"There's no such thing as bad weather, only inappropriate golf clothing… and my swing."

• • •

"I play golf in any weather—that's why they make so many different excuses."

• • •

"Wind is nature's way of making sure every golfer gets to experience British Open conditions."

• • •

"Rain makes the course play longer, but somehow my drives get shorter."

• • •

"The sun was in my eyes… from behind a cloud… at night."

• • •

GOLF PSYCHOLOGY

"Golf is the most fun you can have without taking your clothes off."

• • •

"Golf is a mental game, and I'm severely handicapped."

• • •

"Confidence is hitting a 2-iron into a strong headwind."

• • •

"Golf is like a love affair—if you don't take it seriously, it's no fun; if you do take it seriously, it breaks your heart."

• • •

"The most rewarding thing about golf is that just when you think you've got it figured out, it humbles you again."

• • •

THE 19TH HOLE

"Golf is the only sport where you can drink and drive."

• • •

"The 19th hole is where golf scores improve with each telling."

• • •

"I love golf because it's the only place where 'hitting the bottle' is considered good advice."

• • •

"The best golf stories are told over drinks, and the worst ones are lived on the course."

• • •

"Golf is like whiskey—it's enjoyed best in small amounts and with good friends."

• • •

UNIVERSAL GOLF TRUTHS

"Golf is a game invented by someone who obviously hated people."

• • •

"Golf is proof that God has a sense of humor."

• • •

"The only thing certain about golf is uncertainty."

• • •

"Golf is the cruelest of sports because it offers hope."

• • •

"In golf, as in life, it's not how you drive—it's how you arrive."

• • •

SELF-DEPRECATING CLASSICS

"I'm not bad at golf—I just have a different relationship with par."

. . .

"My golf game is like fine wine—it gets
better with age, but I'm still waiting."

. . .

"I don't play golf to win—I play golf to
not lose by as much."

. . .

"Golf has made me a better person—more patient, more
humble, more creative with profanity."

. . .

"I've been playing golf for 20 years, and I've finally figured
out what I'm doing wrong: playing golf."

. . .

COURSE MANAGEMENT

"The key to golf is managing your misses—mine just
happen to be very well-managed disasters."

. . .

"Course management is knowing which hazard will give
you the best angle for your next shot."

. . .

"I don't play golf courses—I conduct archaeological
expeditions to find my ball."

. . .

"Every hole is a par-3 if you're brave enough."

. . .

"The secret to golf is knowing when to quit—I just
haven't learned when that is."

. . .

PUTTING WISDOM

"Drive for show, putt for dough, chunk for comedy."

. . .

"The difference between a sand trap and a water hazard is
the difference between a car crash and a plane crash—both
are bad, but one's more expensive."

. . .

"Putting is like wisdom—it comes with age, but by then
your hands shake too much to use it."

. . .

"Every putt is straight if you hit it hard enough."

. . .

"The putter is the club with the least
loft and the most blame."

• • •

These classics have survived because they capture the eternal struggle between human aspiration and golf reality. Every golfer recognizes the truth in these jokes—that's what makes them timeless.

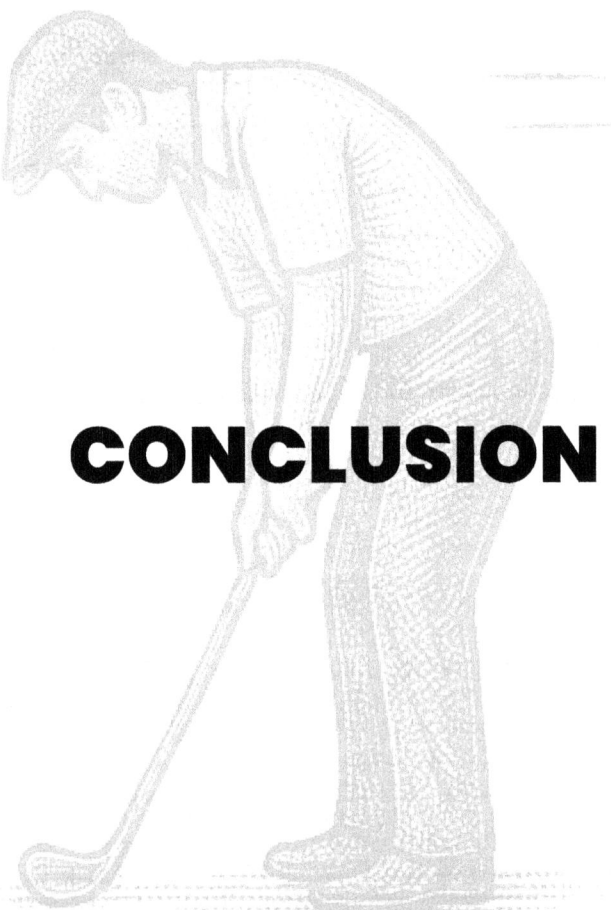

CONCLUSION

Congratulations. You've just completed an advanced degree in Creative Golf Accountability—or more accurately, the complete absence thereof. You now possess the tools, techniques, and philosophical framework necessary to ensure that no golf shot will ever be your fault again.

More importantly, you've discovered that golf's true purpose isn't producing low scores—it's producing high entertainment value. You've learned that the best golfers aren't necessarily the most skilled, but rather the most skilled at making everyone else comfortable with their own lack of skill.

THE TRANSFORMATION IS COMPLETE

When you started this book, you were probably someone who occasionally took responsibility for bad shots. You might have even apologized for poor play or felt genuinely embarrassed about mistakes. That person no longer exists.

You are now a golfer who understands that:
- Weather patterns target your golf ball personally
- Wildlife runs coordinated conspiracy operations
- Equipment has moods and expensive performance issues
- Golf balls make their own poor life choices
- Course designers studied professional sadism
- The universe violates physics specifically for your shots

- AI coaching multiplies problems exponentially
- Golf spending is hope purchases disguised as gear
- Fashion costs increase as golf ability decreases

You've also mastered essential golf social skills:

- Creative accounting for equipment purchases
- Translating disasters into workplace learning opportunities
- Teaching kids excuse-making while staying parental
- Corporate golf diplomacy without career damage
- 19th hole therapy with selective memory enhancement
- Spouse negotiations using golf widow translation skills

This isn't delusion—it's enlightenment. You've achieved the highest level of golf consciousness: the ability to find someone or something else to blame for literally everything that happens during your round.

A FINAL CHALLENGE

As you head back to the course armed with your new arsenal of excuses, quips, and philosophical insights, remember this: your job is no longer to play good golf. Your job is to demonstrate that golf can be enjoyed regardless of performance level.

Show other golfers that it's possible to hit terrible shots while maintaining dignity, humor, and friendships. Prove that the worst rounds can produce the best stories. Demonstrate that taking golf seriously is far less important than taking golf joyfully.

Here's what nobody tells you about golf: the game doesn't care about your score. The course doesn't judge your performance. Your equipment doesn't keep track of your mistakes. Only humans do that, and humans can choose to stop.

Golf is whatever you decide it is. If you decide it's a test of your worth as a person, it will torture you endlessly. If you decide it's an excuse to spend time outdoors with friends while occasionally hitting a ball toward a flag, it becomes exactly that—and suddenly, everything else is just details.

NOW GO PLAY

You're ready. You have excuses for every situation, comebacks for every disaster, and the philosophical framework to enjoy golf regardless of what happens. Most importantly, you understand that golf's absurdity isn't a bug—it's a feature.

So grab your clubs "which may or may not cooperate today", check the weather "which is probably conspiring against you", and head to the course "where the wildlife is waiting to ambush your round".

Remember: whatever happens out there, it's not your fault.

It never was, and it never will be.

Now make sure everyone knows it.

THANK YOU!

Thanks for joining us on this joyful ride through the wild, wonderful world of golf.

If you smiled, chuckled, or found a new excuse worth keeping, then this book did its job.

Your quick review on Amazon helps other golfers discover this little dose of laughter between the fairways.

Because in golf, as in life, the best stories are the ones we pass along.

Leave a review on Amazon

GREENSIDE EDITIONS

REFERENCES

Bailey, R., & Cope, E. "2017". *Engaging young people in golf: A Delphi expert consensus study.* International Journal of Golf Science. https://www.golfsciencejournal.org/article/10464-engaging-young-people-in-golf-a-delphi-expert-consensus-study

Balk, Y. A., Adriaanse, M. A., de Ridder, D. T., & Evers, C. "2013". Keep your eye on the ball: The role of attention in golf putting performance. *Psychology of Sport and Exercise*, 14"2", 248-253.

Boukas, N., & Ziakas, V. "2016". Golf tourists' satisfaction and behavioral intentions: A study in Cyprus. *International Journal of Tourism Research*, 18"4", 322-332.

Breedlove, J., Chen, S. S., Taylor, M., Smith, R., Johnson, L., & Williams, K. "2023". Golfer responses to traditional and technology-enabled equipment sales: A comparative study. *International Journal of Golf Science.* https://www.golfsciencejournal.org/article/90593-golfer-responses-to-traditional-and-technology-enabled-equipment-sales-a-comparative-study

Crawford, S. A., & Caltabiano, N. J. "2011". Promoting emotional well-being through the use of humour. *Journal of Positive Psychology*, 6"3", 237-252.

Data Bridge Market Research. "2024". *Global golf equipment market – Industry trends and forecast to 2031.* https://www.databridgemarketresearch.com/reports/global-golf-equipment-market

Golf Datatech. "2025". *Consumer insights: Understanding golf purchasing behavior.* https://www.golfdatatech.com/consumer-insights/

Gonot-Schoupinsky, F. N., Garip, G., & Sheffield, D. "2020". Laughter and humour for personal development: A systematic scoping review of the evidence. *European Journal of Integrative Medicine*, 37, 101144.

Grand View Research. "2023". *Golf equipment market size, share & growth report, 2030.* https://www.grandviewresearch.com/industry-analysis/golf-equipment-market

Hayslip, B., & Petrie, T. A. "2014". Age, psychological skills, and golf performance: A prospective investigation. *The Journals of Gerontology: Series B*, 69"2", 245-249.

Martin, R. A., & Ford, T. E. "2018". *The psychology of humor: An integrative approach.* Academic Press.

Murray, A. D., Daines, L., Archibald, D., Hawkes, R. A., Grant, L., & Mutrie, N. "2017". The relationships between golf and health: A scoping review. *British Journal of Sports Medicine*, 51"1", 12-19.

Oliveira, R., Arriaga, P., & Barreiros, J. "2023". The role of humor in social, psychological, and physical well-being. *Humor, 36"3"*, 487-509.

Price, K. "2012". A study of golfers in Tennessee. *The Sport Journal.* https://thesportjournal. org/article/a-study-of-golfers-in-tennessee/

Schei, M., Haugen, T., Stenling, A., Grøtting, L. A., Peters, D. M., & Høigaard, R. "2021". Development and initial validation of the humor climate in sport scale. *Frontiers in Psychology*, 12, 696611.

Silvia, P. J., Christensen, A. P., & Cotter, K. N. "2021". If you're funny and you know it: Personality, gender, and people's ratings of their attempts at humor. *Journal of Research in Personality*, 91, 104068.

Stenner, B. J., Buckley, J. D., & Mosewich, A. D. "2020". The association of golf participation with health and wellbeing: A comparative study. *International Journal of Golf Science.* https://www.golfsciencejournal.org/article/12915-the-association-of-golf-participation-with-health-and-wellbeing-a-comparative-study

Torres-Luque, G., Fernández-García, Á. I., & Ramírez-Campillo, R. "2020". Golf tourism and sustainability: Content analysis and directions for future research. *Sustainability*, 12"9", 3616.

Weiss, M. R., Bolter, N. D., & Kipp, L. E. "2016". Evaluation of The First Tee in promoting positive youth development: Group comparisons and longitudinal trends. *Research Quarterly for Exercise and Sport*, 87"3", 271-283.

Wilson, M., Smith, A., & Brown, R. "2019". Consumer decision-making on golf equipment: A behavioral analysis. *International Journal of Sports Marketing and Sponsorship*, 20"3", 412-428.

Printed in Dunstable, United Kingdom

76147553R00107